I Survived the Starr Hill Gang

The True Story of Kids Playing in Wild Alaska

John Bertholl

Publishing Partners
2026

Publishing Partners
Port Townsend, WA

Copyright © 2026 John Bertholl

All rights reserved. No part of this book may be used or reproduced by any means, graphic, electronic or mechanical, including photocopying, recording, taping or by any information storage retrieval system without the written permission of the author except in the case of brief quotations embodied in critical articles and reviews.

ISBN: 978-1-944887-36-0

Cover image from the collection of Doc Eide.

Front cover:
    Gary Baxter (tricycle)
    Freddy Baxter (roller skates)
    Doc Eide, aka Toothless (scooter)
    Johnny Winther (bicycle)

Back cover:
    Mike Freer (bicycle)
    Dale Winther (tricycle)
    Ronnie Baxter (tricycle)

Contents

Ode to the Starr Hill Kids ii
Introduction vii
Dedicated to my friends ix
Big Boots to Fill 1
My First Memory 9
Nobody Cares About Me 13
The Runaway 17
Little Man at the Barber Shop 21
How Blister Got Her Name 29
How Lugnut Got His Name 31
How Spit Got His Name 33
Going Outside 37
The Dump and the Bear 49
How I Learned to Love Clean Dirt 57
How I Gave Myself a Black "DA" 63
A Tinkle in His Eye 69
Catalog Kid 77
Why Alaska isn't in America 83
Buying Muscle 87
Bottom Burp 91
Chocolate Fort 97
Purple Volcano 101
Shore Patrol 107
Firefighters of Starr Hill 111
Fearless and Slightly Confused 121
Devil's Club and Stupid Questions 127
Five Floors, One Gang, Zero Adults 131
How We Got Our News 137
Word of the Day 141
The Blue Bike and the Man Bar 147
Angel Hair and the Devils Itch 153
Not All DA's Are Cool 163
Paratroopers of Starr Hill 169
Cool Cats Give the Finger 177
All in the Word 181
Poop, Feathers and Romance 187
The Big Move 191
Fishing with Lugnut 195
Holy Paddle 203
Epilogue 207
Acknowledgments 209
About the Author 213
Praise for *I Survived the Star Hill Gang* 214

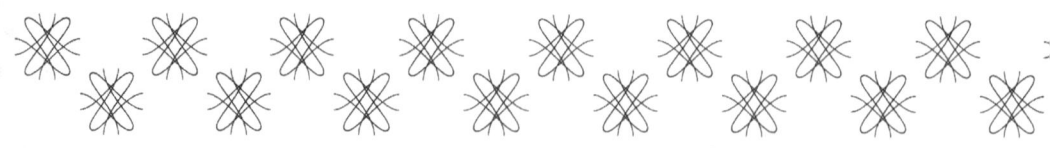

Ode to the Starr Hill Kids

There's a hill above Juneau where childhood hides,
In the fog, the snow and the high-tempered sides.
Where laughter once echoed, through the woods and rain,
There's a gang of small dreamers, being wild once again.

We built forts of rotten lumber and borrowed old nails,
We launched mighty ships, with raggedy cloth sails.
We fought wars with sticks, crowned kings with tin,
And swore we'd grow up—though we never said when.

The street was our kingdom, the woods were our keep,
We guarded our secrets, where the shadows ran deep.
We learned that a scar, was more than a badge,
It proved you survived, the latest hill fad.

We smoked Devil's Club, till our heads nearly spun,
Then promised our mother, we hadn't done none.
We borrowed the truth, as all children do,
And paid it back later, with laughter and glue.

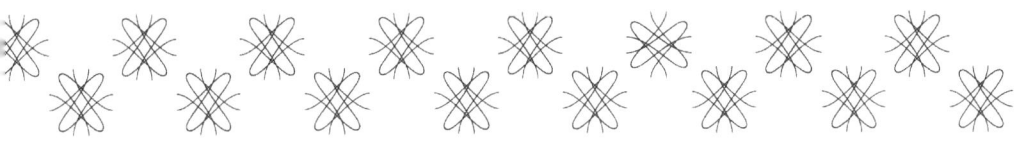

The rain was our drummer, the fog was our veil,
Each story we told grew, just a little more stale.
And though time pulled us down, from that stubborn old hill,
A piece of it clings to our hearts—and always will.

For the tide still sighs, where our footprints fade,
And echoes remember, the games that we played.
If you stand there in silence, you just might hear,
A faint little shout, from a long-ago year.

So, raise your voice and tip your hat,
To every kid who lived like that.
From Mount Roberts' peak, to the Gastineau shore,
We were rich in ways, worth fighting for.

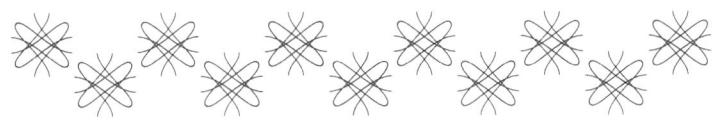

Introduction

For me, memories are like watching a basketball game in a snowstorm. Who's got the ball? Did it go in? Was that a foul or just bad acting? And what's the score again? Things get a little blurry. So, when I write about my early years—starting at four years old—I have to fill in the blanks with what *probably* happened—or what *should* have happened if life had any sense of drama. I may have used my imagination once or twice... okay, maybe three times.

I was born in 1946 in Juneau, Alaska, the territorial capital before we became a state. Back then, it was a small town of about 6,000 folks, and it pretty much stayed that way until Alaska joined the Union in 1958. After that, things started to blossom, though we still had more bars than churches and more fish than people.

Juneau was, and still is, a government town. Lots of offices, some fishing boats, a little construction, and small planes hauling supplies out to the logging camps scattered across Northern Southeast Alaska. It's tucked into the bottom of the state in a stretch called the Panhandle—where the land is lumpy with mountains and stitched together by ocean and ice.

Roads don't get you far around here. From Juneau, you either fly, float, or stay put.

Our town is wrapped in glaciers and rivers, with just two skinny roads poking out. One heads south to a place called Thane, only two and a half miles away—and that's the end of the line. The other called simply "Out the road" goes a grand total of twenty-eight miles before it, too, just... stops. That's Juneau. All roads lead to a dead end. But in between those ends? That's where the story begins.

"That's how it was growing up in Starr Hill. Names have been changed. Guilt has not"

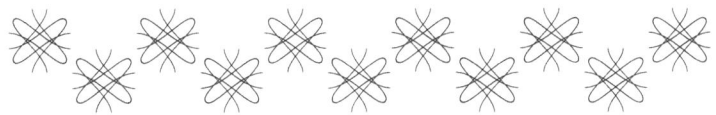

Dedicated to my friends

Karl Schoeppe, who taught me that positive thinking is more than words—it's a way of life.

and

J. Fields, who showed me that believing in the best of others can change the world—one heart at a time.

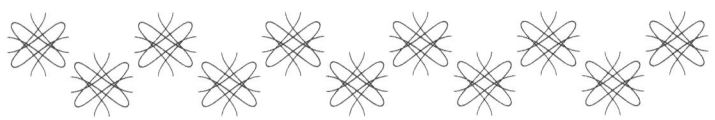

Big Boots to Fill

This isn't just my memory—it's Mom's too. She told it so many times, I could recite it forward, backward, and sideways. It's about the first time I realized my dad wasn't just Dad. He was a fireman. A real one, the kind with boots so big I could fit both my feet inside his one boot and still have room to drive my own pretend fire truck. That's where the story begins.

Back then, Juneau had an all-volunteer fire department. These guys were tough, fast, and proud...and they got paid a dollar for every fire. Fires could last twelve hours or more, but they still showed up. My dad was one of them. When I was maybe four, and even smaller in size, I used to climb into his fire boot. All the way up to my tummy. I'd squat down, peek out the side handles, and then pretend I was barreling down the street with a siren howling... Just like my dad did.

When Dad goes to a fire, he's got a Ford Model A truck that is all black with brown spots. And the brown spots have some holes in them. He also has a really big round red light on top that says STOP. He told me it says STOP. I can't read that big a word yet. But I will when I get to first grade.

When he goes to a fire, he turns the light on and it starts winking: STOP, STOP, STOP. Dad doesn't have to stop. All the other people do. They always stop, and wave at him. He smiles and waves back.

After the fire is out, he comes home. We can hear him clumping up the outside back stairs in his big black fire boots. He always uses the back porch 'cause the front porch stairs are gone 'cause of a mud slide.

Then he goes through the kitchen, then the living room and into the front porch. That's where he puts all his fire clothes.

First, he takes off his hat, big black one, and puts it up near the roof where there's a shelf. Then he takes off his jacket, it's so heavy that if it fell on me I'd never be a fireman or anything else. Sets it all on the floor. Then he takes off that dumb belt that goes over his arms and up around his neck. It's a stupid belt. He lets go of his pants, and they go over his boots. He steps out of them. He leaves all his clothes in the front hall, and they stink like our big burn barrel that we burn garbage in that Dad doesn't want to take to the dump. I like the dump.

Mom should wash his fire clothes. She washes everything. And irons everything. But she doesn't.

My daddy works in a cow shop when he's not at a fire. That's where they cut up cows and make hamburgers and hot dogs. Hot dogs are my favorite. When Dad's at the cow store, I go into the front porch where I climb into Daddy's fire boot and squat down so I can see through those halfmoon handles. They're my side windows. Just like a real firetruck.

"Hey, Mike, you want to go to the fire with me?" Mike's my dog. He sits down beside me on my daddy's fire pants. He loves to pretend he's a fireman hanging onto the back of the firetruck by his feet. Off we go. I'm driving 'cause I'm in the boot and I have the siren. Errr...errr. That's the sound it makes. Mike is scared so he's howling with fear. We do this for a long time. A really long time.

Mom comes and tells me and Mike that some bad outlaws came and stole all our cows and we should go round them up but that we needed to be a little quieter so we can sneak up on them. I climb out of my fire engine boot and go looking for my gun. My brother made a new gun for me from a branch off a tree. Not the whole branch but a part of it. I don't know what part, but it's a really good gun. It's small enough I can stick it in my front pocket. That's where all gunfighters kept their guns. That way you can get it out fast. I'm fast.

I made Mike my deputy. Off we went to round up all the outlaws but he lies down on the rug and starts snoring.

In Juneau not everyone had a phone, so they put some red boxes on telephone poles all over town. Those red boxes had numbers on their front doors. If there's fire, someone that does not have a phone could run over to the red box, pull down the little front door, and then yank the white handle. A string that was hooked to the white handle went all the way down to Fourth Street where the fire trucks slept. Then it ran up a totem pole and out to a big, really big, silver looking horn.

If that horn honked three times, take a nap, and then honked nine more times, that meant there was a fire up on Starr Hill. That's where we lived. Third highest house in Juneau. That's what the numbers on our little red box said, a three and a nine. All the red boxes had numbers on them. Different.

If the horn honks two times, naps, then honked two again, that means all firemen would show up at the fire hall 'cause there might be a fire out the road or someone might be drowning or someone is missing from hunting or there's a emergency on Douglas Island. Two-two means a lot of things.

It wasn't always a emergency. Sometimes they'd blow the horn so the firemen could come down to the fire station and have a beer. Mom told me that. When the fire was out, that big horn would honk two times. That's all. Two times. That told the firemen and everyone in town the fire was out. All the firemen would go back to the fire hall for a beer, then go home. Sometimes. Mom told me that too.

I had a brown coat and green boots that I kept right by my daddy's fire clothes in the front porch. If Daddy was home, and the fire alarm honked, I'd go and put on my fire clothes. Real Fast. I'd be standing by his boots all dressed up ready for a fire.

Dad would come to put on his boots, pull up his pants, and put that dumb belt over his arms. Then he'd put on his jacket and hat. Pat me on "de noggin" and head for the door.

I'd be right behind him. "I can go—I want to be a fireman!"

By the time we got to the kitchen, I'd be crying and screaming, "I WANT TO GO, I WANT TO BE A FIREMAN!"

When Dad went out the back door, Mommy would be standing there, she'd grab me because I was yelling, screaming, and kicking. "You don't love me. I want to be like you." When I heard Dad drive off in his truck, I quit yelling. I go back to playing cowboy. Mike went back to snoring. On both ends.

Someday I had to show Daddy I was big enough to go. I had to go. I was mad at my daddy for not taking me. How could I show him I was big enough? My Dad always told me to use my brain. Maybe I should try.

One day, Dad was at the kitchen table smoking a Camel and drinking his coffee. I was lying beside our big radio in the living room on the hardwood floor, listening to Roy Rogers and Trigger. Sometimes I'd get Roy to go round up a bunch of bad men with me and Mike. I liked him better than Gene Autry, 'cause Gene sings too much and doesn't shoot his gun like Roy.

The fire horn starts honking. Mike and I jump up, but we didn't go into the front porch. We didn't put our fire clothes on and wait for Dad. We snuck into Mom and Daddy's bedroom. We peeked out the door.

Dad went into the front porch and quickly put his fire clothes on. He looked down at my little fire boots. Smiled. But I wasn't in them. He ran through the living room, kitchen and out the back door.

Mom and I were in the living room. Roy Rogers, Trigger and I were back looking for some bad men. Mom was ironing Dad's handkerchiefs. Mike was snoring. Both ends.

We heard the fire horn honk two times, so we knew the fire was out. We know Dad's gonna have a beer and then come home. No beer. I hear his big black fire boots clopping up the back stairs. Then he opens the back door and clomps into the kitchen.

"Aileen! Is Johnny with you!?"

"Yes, dear, we're both in the front room. What do you need?" my mom asked.

"I'd like both you to come into the kitchen."

I grabbed Mom's hand really tight and we walked into the kitchen.

"Please sit down." He wasn't smiling. He always smiles.

We sat down at the old yellow wooden kitchen table. I was shaking.

"What is it Bert? Someone get hurt?"

"No. You know I had fire hall duty this month. By the time I got to the fire hall, I was noticing a problem with my right foot. I started to get a little worried."

"Oh no, Bert. Did you break your big toe?"

"No, no, much worse than that. I knew I had to take off my boot. I sat down on one of the chairs and took my suspenders down and then lowered my pants and took my right foot out of my boot. That's when the problem really started. A few of the guys were standing around and quickly pinched their noses and started laughing, pointing, and commenting that it really must have been scary ride down to the hall. Or do I ever wash my socks. Or what animal crawled into my boot. Their snide remarks and laughter kept coming. A little embarrassed to say the least."

"Oh, Bert, could it have been a mouse?" My mommy said.

I squeezed Mom's hand tighter. Really tight.

My dad walked over to me. He looked down at me. Not smiling. "Son, were you that mouse?"

"Uh-huh."

"And why did you leave me that present?"

"It wasn't a present Dad. It really wasn't. I was mad. I just want to be a fireman like you."

My daddy put his hand on my shoulder very softly. Got down on one knee. "Son, you can't go shitting in my fire boots."

Mom jumped out of the chair. She must have forgotten that we were still connected at our hand. I flew through the air. It's a good thing my feet are on the bottom of my body 'cause that's how I landed.

"Bert, don't use that profanity. John's ears are very tender. He's only four years old. We don't need him to hear that kind of language."

I started tugging on my mom's dress and rubbing my ear.

My mom's voice got faster and louder. My daddy's voice got slower and lower.

I kept tugging and rubbing.

Finally, after a long time of talking, my mom looked down at me. "What is it, honey?"

"I'm 4½. Can I have a peanut butter and jelly sandwich? Maybe Dad would like one too. He can have Mike's."

I turned when I heard the clumping of Dad's black fire boots. I saw them go around the kitchen door then the door closed really loud. All I ever wanted to tell him was: "Someday, I'm gonna fill your big fire boots."

I couldn't wear his boots….
so I made his boots memorable.

Princess Kathleen *ran hard aground on the rocks at Lena Point, fourteen miles north of Juneau, at 2:00 a.m., September 7, 1952. By the afternoon she had slipped off the ledge and settled to the bottom. Remarkably, all 454 passengers and crew survived without a single injury or death.*

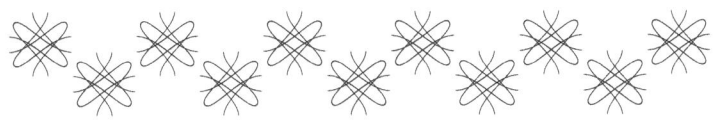

My First Memory

September 7, 1952. I was six years old. This is my first full memory—not parts and bits, not my mom's. But the full-blown picture in my wee little brain.

I heard my dad whispering in my ear. "IF YOU'RE GOING WITH ME, YOU HAD BETTER GET DRESSED AND BE IN THE TRUCK IN FIVE MINUTES!"

Oh boy, Dad's gonna give me a ride to school. Yippee. I jumped out of bed. Picked out my best clothes on the floor and got dressed as fast as a fireman. I ran through the living room, out through the kitchen, then through the back door down the stairs. I jumped into Dad's Model A. Black.

There was Dad. Carla, my sister, was already in the truck. I sat between them. Dad drove. I helped drive too. My brother Wayne was bigger and talked more than Carla and I, so he sat beside the far door. Off we went.

We drove for a long time. "Hey Dad, we missed the school. We better turn around or I'll be late and Miss Murphy will be mad."

"There's no school today. It's Sunday. Pull that blanket up and put it over you and Carla. Take a nap, it's going to be awhile until we get there."

"Where we going Dad?"

"I'll tell you when we get there. Now take a nap."

We must have hit a big hole in the road 'cause my head bounced off the top of the truck. I was rubbing it when I saw cows.

"Look Dad, Sid let the cows out of their house. Can we stop by and say hi to them?"

"We don't have time. Pull the blanket up and go back to sleep."

The next time I woke up there was a big totem pole right in front of us.

"Dad where are we? Don't hit that totem pole."

"Johnny, you finally woke up. We're at the Auke Bay Rec area. Remember?" Wayne said. "They had the Elks picnic here, and you got into a lot of trouble for playing in the Native graveyard."

"I don't think that was me. Sounds like Carla. She's always in trouble, but I get blamed. How much farther we got to go Dad? What time is it Dad?"

"About a mile to go and it's about five thirty in the morning."

The truck stopped. I woke up Carla, and we got out. I followed Wayne 'cause Carla wore those big glasses 'cause she was always reading those stupid books.

"Hey, Wayne. What's all this stuff in the road for? And look, someone built a fire right where they weren't supposed to. How come? Huh?"

"Those are life vests and blankets. Probably came off the ship."

"There's no ship; we're in the woods, Wayne. You're fibbing, and Dad doesn't like us to fib." We kept walking.

Finally, we turned down and walked to the beach. When we got there, I yelled. "Look Dad, there's a boat trying to go up into the woods. Why's he doing that?" That boat was bigger than Sid's cow house. It was bigger than our school. It was the biggest boat I had ever seen.

Dad wasn't anywhere near me. He was talking to a bunch of men about something.

"Wayne," Carla yelled, "why is there smoke coming out of the chimneys? There people still living on it? Or are there ghosts on the boat?"

"No, there's no one on board. And that's the smoke from the water hitting the engines," Wayne said.

We walked a little farther. All of a sudden Carla and I put our hands over our ears. "Wayne, what's that loud screeching?" Sounded like when my friends, Karen and Ruth, ran their fingernails down the black board at school. The boat was moving, slowly and screechy. It slid backwards into the water. Carla was crying. I don't know why, she didn't know anybody on there.

Dad finally came back and stood beside us. "You kids alright?"

"Yeah, I think so. Carla's crying, but she always cries. Was that a real boat wreck?"

Dad said, "Yes, that was a real one. And Johnny, they call them shipwrecks not boat wrecks. The good news is no one died or got injured."

I wanted to ask if I could go on it next time, before it sinks, but maybe now wasn't the time. So I just stood there watching the water bubble, thinking: *this was way better than going to school.*

Funny how some memories sink deep and some never come back up either. Except when you're six, and it's the first one you ever remember.

*Some memories sink—
but this one still floats.*

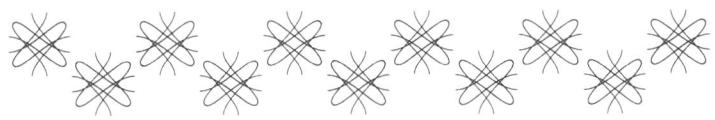

Nobody Cares About Me

We were all sitting around our old yellow wooden kitchen table. There was my mom, my dad, Wayne, and Carla. Oh yea, and me.

We're eating my favorite food tonight, "paghitti."

I'd eat that every day, but Momma says I gotta eat other things. First, she fries up hamburger in a big, really big, iron black pan. Then she gets out the box—the long square one with white noodles. That's what our "paghitti" comes in. Mom puts them in a pan of water that has bubbles all over the top of the water. She waits for a long time, then pours all the bubbling water out and puts the noodles on our plate and covers it with the red stuff. I think it's ketchup. Then Mom takes an ice pick and puts a hole in a little can that was in the box with the noodles and sprinkles the white stuff on top. Oh, it stinks like my daddy's socks but it's really good. Not my daddy's socks. That white stuff.

"Honey," Mom said.

My mom always called me "Honey." She called Dad Bert, my brother Wayne "Honey" and my sister Carla "Honey." But you had to listen closely. Mine came with a smile. Carla's came with a sigh, and Wayne's sounded like "Don't make me come over there."

"Uh-hu!" I said.

"Dad and I have something special for you tonight, Johnny," Mom said.

"Oh, boy. Lemon pie with white stuff on top?"

"No, better than that."

"Chocolate cake an ice cream. Yeah."

"No, tonight you have the honor of washing dishes for the first time," Mom said. "What do you think about that?"

My heart fell to the floor and joined all the little pieces of "paghitti." I've always wanted to wash dishes since I had watched Carla and Wayne do it a thousand times.

Carla slammed her fork on the table.

"Don't do that to us! Wayne and I are quite fine doing the dishes. Let him sweep the floor. Then make him take the dustpan to the garbage dump and empty it. That'll keep him busy until morning."

"Mom. It's July! If we try to teach Johnny to wash dishes, he'll still be trying when there's snow on the ground. I got things to do. I promised Willie I'd help him fix the tire on his bike tonight."

"Hey, you two knock it off. John's going to wash. Carla's going to dry and you, Wayne, are going to clean the table and put everything away. That's final. You both had to start sometime. It's John's turn tonight. Let your Mom and I have a few minutes alone for once."

Dad smiled. "I'll turn the radio on. It's Friday night so *Yours Truly Johnny Dollar* will be on in about twenty minutes. Try to finish up so you can listen," Dad said.

I'd been looking for this moment to happen for a long time. Maybe a month or a year. I was now six and a half, but I looked like I was an old six.

Carla took a square bucket, put it in the sink, and filled it with hot water and some soap she squeezed in. Then Carla got another square bucket and filled it with hot water. I pulled my chair up to the sink, climbed up, then stuck my hands in the dish pan.

Wow, I pulled my hand out of the water and shook them in the air. "Hot, hot, hot."

Carla rolled her eyes like she always does when she talks to me. "Knock it off."

I knocked it off.

I picked up that dish rag and started washing. This was not as easy as it looked when I was sitting at the kitchen table watching Carla and Wayne doing the dishes.

After I washed for a while, bending over made my legs and my back hurt. I needed a break and started to worry I was going to miss my favorite detective, Johnny Dollar. Maybe if I got down quietly and crawled into the living room, nobody would notice I was gone.

"John, if you're going to wash the dishes, you need to scrape the food off first. That's the whole idea of washing dishes. You're not supposed to pretend the plates are boats and the silverware are bombs. Stop doing that or I'm going to tell Mom. And look, there's still food on this plate. Wash it again." Carla was loud.

I quit playing Navy and worked really hard cleaning the dishes. I wanted to get done so I could listen to Johnny Dollar. I wanted to be a private eye just like him. But I needed a gun.

"What are you two knuckleheads doing?" Dad said when he walked into the kitchen.

"Washing dishes Dad," I said with a big smile on my face.

"Not you, those two noodle brains." He pointed to Carla and Wayne. "Don't do that. He's been washing dishes for over an hour now. He's missed Johnny Dollar. No more!"

"What did they do, Dad? Huh? Something bad? Maybe something really bad?"

"Ask your sister, she'll tell you. She's the one who

started this."

Carla and Wayne were laughing so hard they had to hold onto the counter. Tears were running down their cheeks. And they were pointing their fingers at me.

I was mad. I didn't like them pointing and laughing at me.

"What ya do, Carla?"

She finally quit laughing. "After I pretended to dry them, I'd give them to Wayne. He'd sneak around your back then he'd put them in the dirty pile of dishes. You've washed some of those dishes ten times. Don't get mad. Wayne did the same thing to me my first time."

Now they were both sitting at the old yellow wooden kitchen table and laughing. And pointing.

I got down off the chair and ran to my bedroom. Well, not a bedroom but my mommy and daddy's closet. That's where my bed was. I could hear them still laughing. They were laughing at me. Me! They weren't nice. I pulled the covers back and climbed in with all my clothes on. Pulled the blanket over my head. It was dark. I couldn't face my mean sister and brother. They didn't like me, and I didn't like them.

I'll show them. When I get up in the morning, I'm going to run away and not come back. Ever. They'll be sorry. Probably miss me after they know I'm gone.

I was the littlest. But I kept going.

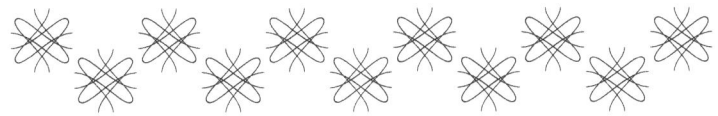

The Runaway

I woke up to the sound of sea gulls. Guess no one heard them 'cause nobody else was up. Good. I could run away without anyone noticing. I don't like being tricked with dishes or being laughed at. I opened the top draw of my dresser and got a pair of white socks out. Then I remembered what my mom always said. "Make sure you have on clean underwear 'cause you never know." I didn't know. So, I grabbed two pair just in case. And a white T-shirt out of the second drawer.

I snuck down stairs and grabbed two pieces of bread and opened the fridge. Took a couple pieces of lettuce. Wrapped the bread in it in case the bread got hard. Now I had food for my tummy. But I needed something to put all my belongings in. I rushed back upstairs and borrowed one of Mom's pillow cases. Put all my clothes and my lunch in it, threw it over my shoulder, and headed out the door. And up the mountain. The last time I ran away I only made it to the tree in the backyard. But this time was for good. I felt like an explorer with my Davy Crockett hat and its long tail following me. Mom read me that story about Davy long time ago.

I walked a long time. Following Mt. Roberts Trail up to the first picnic ground. I laid out all my clothes on the picnic bench. Sat down and ate my bread before it got hard. Didn't know what to do with the lettuce, so I dug a hole and planted it. Maybe they'd grow up and be big lettuce.

I cleaned around the picnic table using a stick for a broom. Clearing out brush, needles, and leaves. I was getting bored and needed to do something. I packed my bag and headed back down the trail 'till I got to 6th street and followed it down Starr Hill. I could hear kids playing in the Chicken Yard, so I turned on Kennedy Street and stood on the wooden bridge where I could watch them playing ball.

That's when Mrs. Cook, who lived just down the street from us, walked by.

"What do you have in the pillow case, Johnny?" Mrs. Cook asked.

"I'm running away from home, and I'm going to show my sister and brother how much they'll miss me."

"Oh. Well... enjoy your trip." Mrs. Cook walked off with a half-smile.

Boy, she didn't seem to care. What's wrong with her?

I didn't see Wayne playing catch in the Chicken Yard, but I did see cousin Hambone. And that cheered me up. A little.

"Hey John, what do you have in the bag?" Miss Bonnie asked as she was walking past me next. She was another neighbor and a school teacher. Not mine.

"I got all my clothes, well, not all of them but most of them, plus two pairs of underwear. My sister and brother don't like me, so I'm running away from home."

"I see. You haven't gotten very far. Where are you headed?"

"I'm not telling. You might tell Carla and Wayne. But I'm going really far. No one will ever find me."

"Okay, I hope to see you back here soon. All your friends...and your Mom... are going to miss you. Be careful now."

That gave me a big worry.

Miss Bonnie was right. Mom's probably worrying herself sick. I wonder if she's called Bernie, the chief of police. Bernie and my mom are always talking words. Mom called it Finnish. I bet she told him I vanished. Maybe I'd better go home and check on her.

I hurried. I couldn't run with my pack, so I walked really fast. I burst into the house. Not a sound. Oh no. Everyone was out looking for me. I walked into the living room. There was my mom ironing Dad's handkerchief.

"Morning, Honey," Mom said. "Did you have a good night's sleep. Carla and Wayne have had breakfast, and they're already outside playing. You want me to fix you some mush so you can go up to your fort?"

I opened my mouth. "Mom?" I couldn't. She didn't even know I ran away. She didn't call Bernie the Chief. She didn't even miss one lettuce leaf. I'd tell her when I got older. It was nice to be back home. Maybe I could wash dishes again tonight.

All I packed was clothes, lettuce, and a lonely heart.

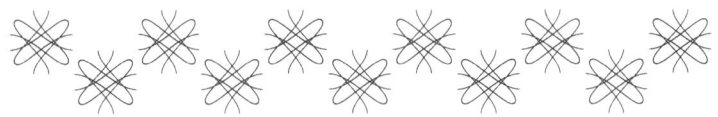

Little Man at the Barber Shop

I never saw my dad get a haircut. He didn't have much hair... Wayne and I had more between us than he did on his whole head. When it was our turn, Mom would always warn us "tonight's haircut night." Like it was gonna be a party. She'd get the scissors, the ones that yanked half your hair out of your head, and then cut the other strands off at different lengths. It looked like Mom put my cereal bowl over my head and cut around it. Only it didn't have any cereal in it.

"Wayne, go jump in the bathtub, wash your hair and don't take too long. Your sister and brother need to take a bath too, and I want Johnny in bed by 8:30," Mom said.

"Why does Wayne always get to take a bath first. I never get to take a bath first. Why can't I take a bath first?" I asked.

"Because you're the smallest and don't need as much water," Wayne said.

"Oh"

"And the dumbest," Carla said.

"But smarter than you Carla." I said. "By a whole little."

Wayne finished his bath, then Carla took hers.

My dog Mike and I sat on the floor listening to the radio. It was 6:30, and the *Triangle Corner* was on. My favorite radio show on KINY.

They told who found a wallet or who hit a telephone pole. That was stupid. And who was overdue from hunting or someone was going to one of the smaller towns. I liked it, 'cause I heard people's names I knew. Sam, the guy with black slick hair and black leather jacket, drove his car into a telephone pole. The pole wasn't damaged, but it caused the lights to go out for a long time. Dad said Sam was in big trouble.

Carla finished her bath, but Mom said I had to wait a few minutes 'cause the water wasn't hot enough on the stove. Our oil stove didn't heat enough water for all three of us to take a bath, so Mom heated up more on top of the stove in big pans. I was always got the leftover water. Brown and full of mystery bubbles. I didn't complain. I just pretended it was the swimming pool. That's why I was last. See? Smart.

"John, go get your clothes off and I'll lay your PJ's on the bed. The water is hot enough. Hurry. I'll pour it in the bathtub right now. It's almost eight o'clock."

Just as I stepped into the bathtub, I heard Dad come through the back door. Mom and he were talking but I couldn't hear what they were saying. I got back out and put my ear to the door. Still nothing. Probably about me. Got back in.

The water was warm. Then Dad walked in.

"Hi son," Dad said. "No hair cut tonight. You and I are going down to the Triangle Club in the morning, and you're getting a real man's haircut. What you think about that?"

Then he sat down on the pot. Wow, a bad, really bad smell took over. I dove under the water. I didn't care how dirty the water was, at least it didn't stink where my head was. I learned to breathe in those tiny air bubbles on top. I was probably under the water for hours. When I lifted my head, Dad had disappeared but he forgot to take that stink with him.

The next morning Dad tried starting the Model A. Nothing. He got his special tool and cranked over the motor until it started. He said some naughty words. Once the motor started, we chugged down Starr Hill over to St Ann's Hospital, down a couple of streets. Then right. Then down. I was lost. Finally, we parked between Nance's Five and Dime store and Lyle's Hardware.

Oh, I hoped I could go in the Five and Dime store. I'd never been in it, but Carla and Wayne had. And they always bought me something. A stick of gum—Juicy Fruit or Black Jack. I loved Black Jack gum because it turned my lips black. And when I gave one to my friend Spit. It made his spit black.

We got out of our old jalopy and then walked down the street to the corner. Dad opened the door. Men. Lots of men. Holding a beer or a glass of something in their hands. Wow. I was in a bar. Not just any bar. The Triangle Club Bar...the one from the radio. We turned left and went into a small room. There was a big, really big chair in the middle. A man had a white apron on, just like the one Dad wore at the butcher shop. He was standing over another man who was sitting in that really big chair. He had a bed sheet on his tummy and had white stuff all over his face. Just like I did once. He didn't smile. I always smile.

"Hey, Bert. That the little man who needs a cut?" Said the really big man holding a sharp knife.

"Yep, that's him Al. I'll be in the other room. Let me know when you're done. John, you can sit down over there on one of those chairs and please don't make a nuisance of yourself. Al will take good care of you."

I sat there, wide eyed. Al took that sharp knife, wiping it back and forward on a big black leather belt. Whoever wore that belt had to be really fat 'cause that belt was really big. Then he pressed his thumb on the blade. He smiled.

He put his hand on the man's head and lifted the knife. I put my hands over my closed eyes. I listened for a scream. I remember when I cut my face, I screamed. This guy is really gonna scream. Nothing. I peeked between my fingers. Al slowly ran that knife down the man's face taking all that white stuff off. He looked better with it off. Then Al took a towel, put it under the hot water spout, and twisted all the water out of it. Smoke was coming off it. He wiped off the man's face, then he took a bottle off the shelf, poured it in his hands, and slapped both the man's cheeks. Smelled like gasoline. Al gave the man a mirror. I don't know if he could see his whole face 'cause it was a small mirror. The man got up out of the chair smiling and gave Al some money. Wow, I knew what I wanted to do when I grew up.

"You want a shave and a haircut or just a haircut?" Al said with a chuckle.

I didn't want a shave, but I couldn't tell him because I was a brave boy. "Whatever my daddy says. But I don't got any money. Only my mommy has money. And she's home."

Al laughed, grabbed a wooden board and put it on the arms of the big chair. "Okey-dokey, up you go."

I climbed up on the chair and sat down on the board. I looked Al right in his eye. We both smiled.

He put a white bed sheet around me and then took out some tape out of a drawer and taped the towel around my neck. He ran his finger through my hair.

"How short you want it? It's Johnny, right?"

"No, it's Johnny Bertholl. I'm my father's son so I got his name too. But his name is Bert Bertholl. Mine's Johnny.

"Whew, glad we got that figured out. Okay, how short do you want it."

"Whatever my dad said. My mom cuts my hair till there's enough on the floor to sweep. Does that help."

"We'll cut the top and clean the sides and make you a handsome lad. How about that?"

"Okay. How much money did you make off that man whose face you washed?"

"You're a clever one. Thinking, that's good. Just relax, and I'll having you looking fine in no time."

Al grabbed a buzzing machine that made my head shake. Like when I put my head against Mom's washing machine. I could see some hair falling on the floor. No scissors, just buzz-buzz-buzz. When Al was done, he handed me a mirror. I looked in it and saw me. Nothing different. Was I handsome? Maybe. What a stupid mirror.

I got down off the chair and went into the bar looking for Dad. I found him playing cards.

"Hey, Dad, I'm done."

My Dad looked up from his cards and his jaw dropped down like he saw a ghost. It was only me. Handsome.

"Here's twenty-five cents. Go over to the Five and Dime and buy something. Come back in about an hour and then we'll go home."

I'd never gone into a store by myself. I pushed the heavy door open and stood there staring. Wow.

How do I find anything? There are too many things. Slowly I walked down a hallway. Did Dad know I could buy all this stuff with my twenty-five cents?

I stopped in front of some small cars and trucks. I liked the blue ones.

"Can I help you find anything?" an old woman asked me.

"My Dad gave me twenty-five cents. His name is Bert, and he's in the Triangle Club. Told me I could buy something. But there are too many things."

"Well, what's your name?"

"John, but if I'm bad, it's John Harold. I'm a good boy today."

She smiled, "Well, John, we've got candy, gum, baseball cards...take your time."

I liked her. She was a nice lady. Carla and Wayne always buy me gum, maybe I'll get them some.

I walked up to the front and the lady was standing there smiling. I think she was smiling at me.

"I got twenty-five cents. Can I have some gum for my brother and sister. They are older than I, so bigger pieces".

"That's sweet of you. Gum's five cents a pack. You could get a Juicy Fruit, Black Jack, and maybe five Bazookas. They've got comic strips inside. And you get a dime back."

"Wow, I never had bubble gum."

"What kind of gum would you like?"

"Could I please have a Juicy Fruit and a Black Jack. Oh, yea, and five Bazooka's. Do I still get my twenty-five cents back?"

She laughed. "Just a dime."

"Oh boy. Can I come back tomorrow too?"

"That you'll have to check with your Dad. I'll put them in a little bag for you. Maybe you better head back to the Triangle Club and let your Dad know you're alright. He's probably worried."

I walked back to the bar with my little brown bag of gum. I could hardly wait to see Carla's and Wayne's faces when I give 'em that gum. Dad was sitting in the same chair and had the same cards in his hand.

"Hey Dad, got Carla and Wayne some gum. Let's go home now."

"You know how to get home on your own?" he asked. I could barely understand what he was saying 'cause his lips kept spitting out his words.

"Yea." It wasn't dark so I knew how to get home. On my way home, I stopped and told my good friends Bingo and Bones about my haircut and the Triangle Club.

I think my dad forgot how to get home 'cause it was dark out when I heard him and my mom talking loudly why it took him so long to get home. And did he forget he had a son.

I'll never forget sitting on that board looking Al right in the eye when he called me "little man."

That's still me. I'm a short man.

*A haircut, a barstool, and
five Bazookas later, I was a little man.*

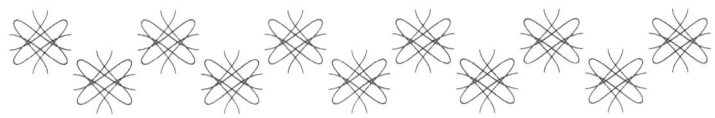

How Blister Got Her Name

Carla, that's my bigger sister. She's three years older than me but that doesn't mean she's smarter. She's just taller.

We were down in the basement trying to build a bird house, like the one we saw in the *Look Magazine*.

"Ok, you draw the dumb bird house, then I'll build it," I said. "But draw it so I can put a piece of wood over it and follow the lines," I said.

"How stupid are you? If you put a piece of plywood over my picture, you can't see it."

"Let's forget that stupid bird house and get some nails and pound them into a board that's more fun. And birds don't come into the basement anyway," I said.

"Okay, you get the nails. I think they're under Dad's workbench. I'll get some boards."

Dad sure has a lot of nails. Some were big ones. Bigger than the boards. I don't think Carla can even pick one up.

"I'll find some little ones both of us can hammer," I said. I took out a coffee can full of nails. Little ones and ones a little bigger than little.

"Hey, I got the nails and big hammer. I'm gonna use both arms to swing this thing."

Carla came over with two pieces of wood and put them on the floor. Dad's work bench was too high from the ground. We got down on our knees, and put a piece of wood between us.

"I go first," I said. "Men are carpenters."

"You're not a man. You're a little boy with baggy pants. I'll go first."

She picks up a nail, point down with her thumb and first finger. Then lifts the hammer with one hand and swings at the nail. Bang!

You could hear her scream in China. That's where all the starving kids live. Dad told me that at dinner.

She ran upstairs bawling, "Mommy, Mommy! My finger's broken."

Mom sat her down in the chair by the kitchen table. I wanted to see it. I'd never seen a broken finger before. I was excited.

Mom took Carla's hand and held it out. "It's not broken honey, but you're going to have a huge blister."

"Let me see! Let me see," I yelled.

There was a big, really big, red and black bubble growing on her left thumb. Wow, it kept growing. It looked like it might pop, or maybe bounce. Wonder if it could grow as big as Wayne's basketball?

"Sit still, Honey," Mom said. "We'll pop it, so you don't hit it again and get blood everywhere."

Blood, oh boy, blood. I loved blood.

Mom held her hand. Taking one of her sewing needles she stuck it into the black and red bubble of blood. Red blood shot out as high as the ceiling. Almost as high. I think it was that high. Maybe higher. She didn't even cry. She was a strong girl. She was part of the Starr Hill Gang and we don't cry. I really liked my sister.

*One thumb, one hammer, and
one brother who never let her forget it.*

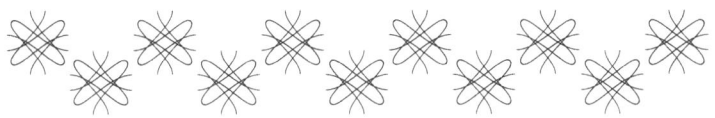

How Lugnut Got His Name

Wayne, that's my brother, who's three years older than Blister, and Blister's three years older than I. So, Wayne is really old. And big.

I wasn't allowed to go in his room. Ever. If I even peeked in, he'd yell, "Move it!" I never found "it," so I didn't know what to move. I'd just go back downstairs and bug Mom.

Wayne had this box in his bedroom, and I'd see him putting something in it once in a while. I had to find out. But he'd never let me in, so finally I got brave and asked him.

"Hey Wayne, what you got in that box that you're always putting something in. Huh? Is it something we can eat together? Can I look and see? Huh?"

"You been peeking through my door?"

"I'm not superman, wish I was. I saw you when your door was open. Can I look in the box? I won't tell Blister or Mom. Please, with sugar on it."

"Come on." He let me in his room for the first time since I was born. Wow! He had pictures of cars all over his walls. I didn't know there were so many different cars. I knew which one I wanted. The blue one.

He took off his coat that covered the big crate box and lifted the lid. Inside there were hundreds, maybe a thousand, of nuts.

"What you gonna do with all those nuts?"

"Those aren't just nuts," he said. "Those are lug nuts. They hold the wheels on a car."

"Yea, but where's the car?"

"That's the point. When I get that box filled with lug nuts then I'm going to go out and buy a car. It's like a...a how do I say it in your language. It's like a wish. You understand now?"

"You got a box of lug nuts holding the wheels on a wish that doesn't have a car yet. But someday the wish turns into a car, and then you've already got the lug nuts. Right?"

He started laughing. "If you say it that way, exactly."

From then on, I called him Lugnut...because he had all the nuts, and maybe someday, if I get a wish, he'll give me some so mine can come true.

He had a box full of nuts and a little brother who was missing a few.

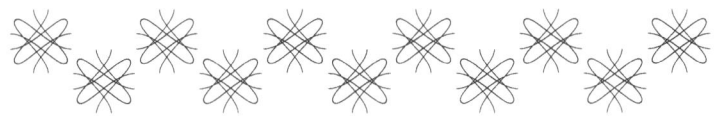

How Spit Got His Name

My dog Mike and I were curled up with a heavy blanket over us and our bottoms were right against the oil stove. Our bottoms were warm and so were we. Nothing gonna move us.

"It's cold outside, Mike. Mom says it's five degrees." Mike went everywhere I did, except he wouldn't get in the bathtub with me. I don't think he could swim. It was okay 'cause I could dog paddle for both of us.

Knock-Knock.

"There's someone at the back door, could you check, honey?" Mom yelled from upstairs. When she said "honey," she meant me.

I piled my blanket on Mike and opened the door. It was Roddy, one of the Starr Hill Gang.

"Roddy, what you doing. It's freezing out. Get in."

Roddy and I went into the living room and sat down by the stove putting the blanket over the three of us.

"Let's go sledding. No one's on the hill. We can make a snow jump and we'd be all by ourselves," Roddy said.

I thought about it for a time. "Yea, let's do it. Can I use your Silver Streak. I hope I got one for Christmas. You can use my old slug."

Roddy was all dressed. I had to go and put on my winter clothes. I reached into my drawer and got out two pairs of pajama bottoms and put them on, then I put my jeans over them. I put on two flannel shirts, blue and green, red and yellow. Then my heavy wool jacket. Now all I had to do was find some wool socks for my feet and two pairs for my hands.

"Don't forget to put your stocking cap on. And come in before you start shaking," Mom yelled.

Out the door we went.

Roddy had a bad habit…he spit. His father spit too, but his spit was a dirty brown color. Roddy's was clear, except when he had a cold, then it was green and yellow. And he had a cold.

We sledded for a long time. Roddy said he was getting cold feet. Pulling our sled back up the hill for the last time, I looked at Roddy's jacket. He had a glacier hanging off of it. Green and yellow glacier. I hated looking at it. Every time he spit, I wanted to see how much bigger it grew.

"John, could you help me unzip my jacket? My mom will give me a spanking if I come into the house with stuff on my zipper."

I wanted to say no. My stomach started to turn around in my tummy with the thought of touching that icky-icky mess. I was wearing sox gloves with no thumbs, so I figured I could handle it.

"Okay, wait here. I'll be right back."

I ran up to our basement and grabbed a screw driver and a hammer. Then I ran back down to where Roddy was shaking. He was cold or afraid of getting a spanking.

"Lay down in the snow on your back and hold this screw driver in the center of your icky glacier."

"What ya gonna do?"

"Don't worry. But don't move. I'm goin' hit that screwdriver with the hammer and the icky ice will fall apart."

Roddy was so cold he was shivering. "You done this before?"

"No, but I saw my dad break some ice off of the railing, and it really worked good. Don't worry, I'll try to hit the screw driver."

Roddy didn't know it, but I was shaking too. I never hit a screw driver on someone's chest. And maybe I'd miss. Then I thought that's okay, 'cause if I miss, all I'm gonna do is hit the ice. Yea. I lifted the hammer and lowered it slowly on to the screw driver.

Nothing.

I did it again. A little faster. And again. A little harder. Finally, it broke in half.

"Roddy, open your eyes. It's gone. Your safe. That wasn't bad."

Roddy let out a sigh, like he'd survived a war.

"From now on," I said, "I'm calling you Spit."

I only gave three nicknames: Blister, Lugnut, and Spit. The rest of the gang showed up pre-labeled.

And that's the day Roddy became Spit.
Some kids earn their nickname. He... grew his.

Going Outside

"Mommy, there's someone at the door. I'm busy doing what you told me to do. Putting all my clothes in that big blue bag."

I heard Mom answer the door. "John, your friends are here to say good-bye."

Standing on the porch stood Bones, Spit and, Nancy—three proud members of the Starr Hill Gang.

"You going on an airplane to America tomorrow?" Bones asked.

"Yeah."

"Hey, could you get us a snake? I've only seen one in the movies. And that was at the Capital Theater," Bones said.

"Yeah."

"Could you bring me back one of those bees. I love bees. They're supposed to be a lot bigger than our bees," Nancy said.

"Yeah, what do want, Spit?" I asked.

"Nuttin," Spit whispered.

"I'll get you all something if I can. See you when I get back."

I shut the door and ran upstairs to finish putting my swimming suit in the bag. That's all I needed. I was ready.

The next morning my whole family was at the Juneau Airport. Blister was over by the big windows. "Here it comes," yelled Blister jumping up and down. Just like a girl.

A bright shiny silver plane that looked like one of Card's pop cans with wings on it was driving up the road. I loved Card's pop; it was made in Juneau. The plane was bigger than a PBY or a Grumman Goose. These were planes that could land on the water or at the airport. I loved to watch them land on the water in front of the Standard Oil Dock. I could see them from our house. I'd watch them all day if I didn't have to work on our fort!

Pacific Northern was written on the side of the plane. That's what Mom told me 'cause that's a big word. I couldn't read that good. Yet. On the back of the plane, on the wings that stuck up in the air, someone wrote PNA on them. The middle wing that went up and down had an Alaskan flag. It had four big huge engines. Lugnut said the airplane is called a Constellation or "Connie" for short. I wonder why they didn't call it Nancy or Sue. I knew both of those girls.

A big man pushed some stairs up to the side of the plane. Then part of the plane fell open and a funny looking lady, all dressed in blue, stepped out onto the stairs. She had a really funny hat on. I wouldn't wear a stupid hat like that.

People came down the stairs and into the airport. Mom and Dad said hi to almost everyone that got off that plane. They sure knew a lot of people.

Some of the men stopped and asked Dad, "You going outside?"

"Yea, Aileen and the kids are headed to Portland to see Aileen's mother."

I know we have to go outside to get on the plane but why does everyone ask Dad that stupid question.

"Hey, Lugnut, why do all those people keep asking Dad if we're going outside. We got to go outside to get on the plane. Kind of stupid isn't it."

"No, that's not what they're saying. When you say you're *"going outside,"* it means you're going to the lower forty-eight. Like Seattle or Portland or somewhere in America.

It didn't make any sense. Why don't they just say we're going to America.

I was getting excited. A man stood by the front door of the airport and opened the door, putting a stick under it to keep it open. Now all the mosquitoes could come in and bite us. How stupid.

"Flight 64 to Annette Island and Seattle is now ready for boarding. Please extinguish all cigarettes and refrain from smoking till the *NO SMOKING* light goes off in the cabin. Hand your ticket to the agent at the door. Thank you and enjoy your trip. We look forward to serving you again."

Mom gave Dad a big kiss goodbye then turned around and handed the man at the door some papers. Following Mom, we climbed the stairs to the plane. Boy, is this thing big. I wonder if the lady with the funny hat is flying the airplane.

"I want to sit by the window!" I said.

"No, I want to. He always gets what he wants. Besides he's too little to know what's going on. And I'm a lot smarter than him," Blister said.

"Okay, okay. Remember we're not going to fight on this trip. John is sitting by the window till we get to Annette Island. Then you can sit by window all the way to Seattle. Can you both agree to that?" Mom asked.

"Yeah."

"Okay, but I don't want to sit by him. I want to sit by you mom," Blister said.

I sat down in this big chair. It was blue. Maybe gray, but I liked things that were blue. I put my nose to the window. I heard the door close. I could see them wheeling the stairs away. I hoped they had some more stairs in Annette. I didn't think I could jump that far to the ground. Maybe I could, but I knew Blister and Mom couldn't.

A voice from the ceiling or maybe under the floor, announced, "Good afternoon ladies and gentlemen. Welcome aboard Pacific Northern Airlines Flight 64 Constellation service to Seattle with an intermediate stop at Annette Island. Your flight is under the command of Captain Eide and your stewardess in the forward cabin is Miss Reynolds. I am Miss Komatsubara. We will be serving you lunch after we leave Annette Island on our final leg to Seattle. Please let us know if there is anything we can do to make your trip more comfortable."

"May we remind you to place your seat backs in an upright position during take-off, fasten your seat belt, and refrain from smoking until the signs have been turned off. Thank you."

She must be beautiful, 'cause she sounds like she should be.

Suddenly, a loud whining noise pierced my ears. Grabbing my seat, I looked around the plane. Mom pointed out the window. I looked out. One of those big engines began to turn. Slowly. Then faster. Bang, bang, poof. Black smoke poured out of the engines. Oh, no, we're on fire. Now the engines were going around and around so fast I couldn't see it. Part of the wing started going up and down. Like it was waving goodbye to someone. Maybe Dad. Then the next engine did the same thing. I could smell gasoline just like when Dad filled the Model A at Juneau Motors. I forgot to breathe. Blister had her dress over her eyes. Lugnut, sitting across from us, seemed to be smiling. I should have sat next to him.

The plane started to move. Then it stopped. It turned around. Guess we we're going the wrong way. All of a sudden the engines started going faster and faster. Then the plane shook. My seat shook. I shook. I looked at my mom. She shook. We started to move forward. But a lot faster. I hoped we were going the right way this time because we were going too fast to turn around again.

The building where we left Dad went whizzing by. I was afraid to look outside. When I did, we were in the air. I looked down. There was Smith's Dairy. All the cows looked up at us. We were flying. Holy cow. I love this.

The "No Smoking" light went off. Everyone lit cigarettes except Mom, Blister, Lugnut, and me. Slowly, I could see layers of blue and white smoke rising to the ceiling. I wished someone would open the window to let out some of that smoke. I wanted to cough, but didn't. I didn't care. I was flying high.

We flew right over Juneau. I could see our house on Starr Hill. I waved hoping the gang might see me. Higher and higher. Now we were as high as Mt. Roberts and Mt. Gastineau. They were covered in snow. I could see clouds out the side of plane. Still going up. We were higher than the earth. We flew right into those clouds. I didn't hear anything when we hit the clouds. All at once, I couldn't see a thing. It was like being under my bed sheets without a flashlight. Then blue sky.

The clouds below looked like the tiny cotton balls my mommy puts in my ears when they hurt. I wanted to step out the door and walk on them. I probably shouldn't. I wouldn't know when the next plane might show up.

"Coffee, tea, or milk?"

It was the lady with the funny blue hat. She had wings on her jacket and the whitest teeth I'd ever seen. Was she a pilot? I didn't think girls could fly.

"Who's flying our plane," I asked.

"Mr. Eide is our pilot. Would you like some wings to put on your chest?" she asked. She was beautiful.

"Oh boy, yes, please! Could you give my sister one too? I call her Blister but you can call her Carla."

"Of course." She smiled. My face got hot.

Blister and I thanked her and then Mom asked for some coffee and said that my sister and I would like some milk. Lugnut, still smiling watching the engines go around, said he'd like some coffee.

That voice came out of nowhere again. "Please fasten your seat belts and refrain from smoking until you're well inside the terminal at Annette Island. We will be landing in ten minutes."

Down we went. Back through the clouds. I like riding on top or below them. I couldn't see when we were in them, and I wondered if the pilot could. Maybe he just closed his eyes till we went through them.

The engines were making a lot of noise. Faster-slower-faster. I could see land coming up. Fast.

Then we hit something or something hit us. I bounced in my seat. Three times. We were driving down a road again. My stomach was in knots. We stopped. Then turned around and headed the other way. Finally, we stopped.

"We've arrived at Annette Island" the pilot said. "If your destination is Ketchikan, you will be able to catch a connecting flight from here. All passengers must disembark. For those continuing on to Seattle, we will be on the ground thirty to forty minutes. We hope you enjoyed your flight, and we look forward to serving you again."

When we took off from Annette Island heading to Seattle, Blister was sitting by the window. I didn't really care about flying anymore. She always takes the fun away from me.

We arrived two hours later in Seattle. We had to wait for another plane to fly to Portland. Mom's Mom lived there. In Portland.

I never met Mom's Mom before, but she had to be old. Mom was old, so how old could her mom be? I bet really old. When we got off the plane in Portland, a little old bow-legged lady, not much taller than I, came up and gave Mom a big hug and kiss.

Mom was all smiles. Mom introduced each of us to her. All I know is her name is Grandma. She didn't speak as good as I did. Mom said she was Finnish and still had the Finnish tongue. I didn't want to see it.

We left the Portland Airport and headed to Grandma's house. Grandma drove. I don't know how. She was so short she sat on a pillow so she could see over the steering wheel. Now her legs barely reached the pedals on the floor. I'd been with Dad enough to know one pedal made the car go and the other made it stop, and the third peddle was for nothing. She didn't have a third peddle. I watched her feet the whole way to her house. We made it to her house, and I knew I didn't want to ride with her anymore.

Grandma had a television. Something that Blister and I had never seen. We didn't like it 'cause you had to sit inside and do nothing except watch a black and white picture. Stupid. Mom and Grandma would sit for hours, watching and talking. They'd have coffee, and Grandma would take a square of sugar and put it in her mouth. When she was all done with her coffee, she'd take it out and put what was left of that square sugar, in a little dish. I couldn't take my eyes off of her. I wanted to drink coffee, but they said I was too young.

Every day Blister and I played in different yards. Grandma's yard. Then the neighbor's yard. Then back to Grandma's. I missed home. We never saw Lugnut. He was much older so he could go to Janzen Beach and other places by himself. Places we couldn't go.

I decided I had to branch out. Do something on my own. I headed out the door. Telling everyone I'd be back in an hour. I walked to the corner. Wow! The cars zoomed by. There must be hundreds of them. I just stared. Finally, I figured I'd better get back home because a bunch of hours had gone by.

I walked into Grandma's house, and Blister said. "You get scared? It's only been ten minutes since you left." She was giggling. Like she always does.

I went up to where my bed was and lay down. They didn't understand. I was worried about them. I wasn't scared. It was so hot. The radio said it was eighty degrees. It never got that hot at home. I needed to go back. It never rained here at all.

Sunshine, then more sunshine. Yuck.

A few days later I found it. I was on one of my big walks. It was green with a funny design down its back. I stepped back. I stared at it then ran to Grandma's. Got a jar with a turn top on it and raced back to where it was. It hadn't moved. I wasn't scared. I took off the top and got down on my knees. I was trying to get it in the jar when a car horn blasted.

"Hey, kid. Don't play in the street. You'll get run over."

"Okay, soon as I get this snake in my jar."

He laughed and drove on.

I ran home.

"Blister, Blister, I did it."

"What did you do now?" she asked. "Are you going to be in trouble?"

"No, I got myself a snake. It's not really for me. I'm taking it home to Bones." I held up the snake in the jar towards her.

"John, how stupid? That snakes been run over. It's dead."

"I know. You think I want to take a live snake on the plane. What if it gets sick? No, I'm taking this one."

Now all I had to do was get a bee for Nancy, then I could go home.

The next day, Blister spotted bees in Grandma's back yard. Whoopee. I went inside and grabbed another jar with a turn lid. I raced outside and found the most beautiful yellow and black bee I ever seen. It was huge. I took the lid off the jar and when the bee sat on a flower, I put the jar over it and slammed down the lid. I screwed it tight.

"You better put some holes in the lid of that jar or your bee will die," Blister said.

"You gonna help me, Blister?"

We went to Grandma's basement. I found a nail and hammer and gave them to Blister. She put four holes in the lid. Back upstairs we went. We went outside. I set the jar on the table and watched the bee. He was a busy bee. You could hear him buzzing. He didn't like being in a jar. I talked to him, trying to calm him down. I told him he was going on an airplane. A PNA airplane.

After a while he calmed down. I slowly unscrewed the lid. I put my finger in to pet him. He must not have recognized me 'cause a terrible pain shot through my finger, up my arm to, my brain. I dropped the jar and ran to the couch crying. Mom was knitting but turned to help.

"What's your problem?" Grandma asked. I told her about the bee. She shook her head back and forth. Grabbing my hand, she brought me to the kitchen and put my finger under the cold-water spout. She turned to Mom and said, in her funny way of talking, "Is he a relation to you?" Then laughed.

"Johnny, in Finland, little boys don't cry. If they hurt somewhere, they ask for a cup of coffee."

"Could I please have a cup of coffee? With a square of sugar? I won't cry."

Grandma got a small cup, kind of like Blister's, the ones she has a tea party with, and poured some of her coffee into my cup.

I put the square of sugar in my mouth. It tasted so sweet. I lifted the cup of coffee to my lips and took a gulp. Hot! I spit it out—coffee and sugar. I picked the sugar square off the floor, brushing it off and put it back in my mouth, but I never again asked for Finnish coffee.

Later I asked Mom if we could go inside.

"Honey, we are inside. What do you mean?"

"When we left Juneau, everyone said we were headed outside. Lugnut told me that meant coming down to this stupid place. I want to go home. I want to go back inside."

Back to Juneau we headed. One snake. No bee, but I got a lump where the bee bit me, and I can show the gang. I had enough of those PNA airplanes. I hope it's raining in Juneau. I wonder if the Starr Hill Gang will be waiting at the airport for me.

I'm never going outside again.

Next time someone says "go outside," I'm locking the door.

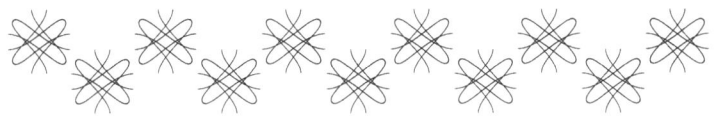

The Dump and the Bear

Dad was cleaning the basement, like he always does when he's home.

"You catching any flies?" Dad asked with a big smile.

"Huh?"

"You're standing there with your mouth wide open. A seagull could fly in there and lay eggs."

"I was thinking, Dad. Can we go to the dump? Huh?" I asked.

The dump was the most important place in our little lives. If you had a trip to the dump, you'd have a big story to tell the other gang members at the fort. Wherever the fort is on that day. The dump was my favorite place.

"You ask me that every day. Do you think our house is so full of garbage that we have to go to the dump every day?" Dad said in his very calm voice.

"I'm just thinking it's time. Mom is always throwing things away, so we must have a whole bunch of garbage by now."

"Your mom doesn't throw anything away. I sometimes wish she would. But if you clean that room of yours, I think by the weekend we'll have enough garbage. Then we can go. How's that sound."

"Oh, goody, how many more days till the weekend?"

"Three more days."

"What day is the weekend?"

"Saturdays. Don't you have something to do?"

"Yea, I'm going up to the fort with Bones. See ya Saturday, Dad."

I woke up Saturday morning all excited. Dump day. I could hardly wait. Dad had his Model A parked out front. It had a big red light on top that said STOP 'cause he was a real fireman, and I was gonna be just like Dad.

He was throwing branches and junk into the back of the truck. I had to hurry so I could help him.

I ran down the stairs where Mom was washing dishes.

"Honey, where you going in such a hurry?" Mom asked.

"Got to help Dad put garbage in the truck 'cause him and me are going to the dump. Just me and him. No one else."

"Not before you have something to eat. How about some mush or Quaker Oats? Don't worry, your Dad's not going to leave without his helper."

"Can I have a piece of toast and some blueberry jam on it? That's all cowboys eat when they're chasing outlaws. Huh?"

Mom fixed a piece of toast with and blueberry jam. I grabbed it and out the door I went. I stuffed the toast in my coat. Now I could help Dad.

We loaded up some boxes of beer bottles and tar paper. Dad lifted the heavy stuff. I showed him where I would have put it. And he did. He threw our two gray garbage cans on top of the pile. They were heavy. Then he took a rope and tied it all to the truck. My dad sure knew how to do lots of things. And he knew how to tie a lot of knots. He always told me if I didn't know how to tie a knot to tie a lot. Then he'd laugh.

"Hop in, we're headed out. We don't have all day," Dad said smiling. He always smiles.

Down Starr Hill we went. We live in the third highest house in Juneau, Alaska. Driving down by St. Ann's Hospital, then down a couple of more streets. Wow, I almost knew how to get there, but not all the way. We were now on the flat streets heading for the City Café. My good friend Karen's parents owned it. We drove by there, then by a huge metal fire box. It was really big and shaped like a rocket ship. It glowed red it was so hot. Dad said they burned all the wood that they couldn't sell. They called it Columbia Lumber. We kept driving.

Dad said if we continued on out past the dump, we'd run into Thane, that's where he lived when he was a small boy. We passed the rock dump. Not the same as the dump. No, the rock dump was where all the rocks from the AJ Mine that didn't have gold in them anymore were buried. Most of Juneau was built on AJ rock. My dad said that too. There were railroad tracks and small houses on it and a bunch of old cars. Dad said it was all junk. I didn't want any more junk.

I squinted my eyes. Was that it? I thought I saw one but wasn't sure. We kept driving. Dad drove into the dump and parked right in the middle of a big mud puddle.

"Don't go far from the truck. I mean it. Remember what's out there," Dad said.

I jumped out of the truck and the smell almost

made me jump back in. Wow. How do people stand having all this stinky garbage in their houses?

While he threw all the garbage out of the truck, I walked very slowly towards the other side of the dump. There were mud puddles everywhere, but it didn't matter 'cause I had on my green boots. My big cousin Hambone told me a little boy walked into a mud puddle and disappeared. Never saw him again. Hambone said sometimes there's a hole in the bottom of the mud puddle. I stopped before I got to the middle of the puddle. I poked the bottom of the mud puddle with my foot looking for a hole. I couldn't find one so I kept walking. The puddle was almost over my boots.

All of a sudden a pile of the dump started to slowly move. The pile of garbage stood up. I froze. The garbage shook. I froze more. Then I saw it. There was a small brown bag of something hanging from his mouth. He was almost gray from that stinky garbage, but I knew he was a black bear. I walked backwards. It hadn't seen me yet...I hoped! I stopped. My butt ran into something. My heart felt like it was flying away. Far away. Without me. I tried to get some air in my tummy.

"I told you not to go too far!" It was Dad I had backed into. "Let's go sit in the truck and watch that black bear. It'll be a lot safer. There's more of them out there. That's why I didn't want you going too far. They're more interested in eating their lunch than you. But they might think you're trying to steal it. That could change their mind."

I wouldn't think of eating that junk. I can't stand the smell, and I is a lot smarter than that stupid bear.

We climbed into the Model A and looked out the

front window of the truck as the bear went through bag after bag and box after box. He'd peek over at us once in a while then go back to munching on something. I could stay there all day and watch, but Dad said we had to get home, so Mom won't worry.

We were just about to leave when Dad poked my arm. I jumped. I wasn't scared. Just like to jump. A mommy bear with two little bitty bears walked toward the truck. Then she stood up on her two back legs and looked around. Her little babies stood up just like their mom. She saw that other bear eating garbage. She dropped back down and started walking with her kids. She had been standing in the same place where I run into Dad. The very same mud puddle. I'm glad I'm not there now. She's bigger than me.

"Dad, we better get out of here or that momma bear is gonna eat us."

"Just sit still and be quiet. She saw that other bear, and she's going to get her cubs out of here before that male bear comes over and kills them."

"Why would he kill them? They're cute. I bet they're nice too?"

"That's how bears live. Don't worry. Momma bear will protect those two cubs with her own life."

We watched as they waddled across the dump. They were kind of running. It looked like their bottoms were trying to pass their front end. It was funny, and I was laughing. Finally, they crossed Thane Road and headed up Mt. Roberts. We lived on the other side of Mt. Roberts. Wow, I hope they come down to Starr Hill and visit us. I liked her kids.

As we drove out of the dump, someone Dad knew

drove in. At least they waved at each other.

On the way home, I did most of the talking. But with Dad, that was always the way it was. He hardly talked.

Finally, he said, "You know we're going to have a flat tire when we get home, so you better keep your work clothes on so you can help me change the tire."

He always got a flat tire when we went to the dump. You'd think he could miss those holes.

I reached into my jacket and pulled out the piece of toast Mom made for me. Brushing off the mud and rocks, I showed it to Dad. "Dad, you want part of my jelly and toast Mom made?"

"Thanks, but you need it more than I do." He was smiling.

"Thanks, Dad."

I ate the whole thing. I was hungry from doing all the work.

Black bears spent most of their time up Mt. Roberts and didn't bother anyone. But a few times a year, one would walk downtown just to see what was going on. In the fall they always came down and got into our garbage cans on the back porch. It happened at night. Our back door had a big window in it so we'd watch a bear carefully go through everything. It would glance up now and then just to make sure we were watching.

Mom got out the camera and put one of those round clear bulbs in a silver shaped bowl. She waited till the bear looked our way. A bright light came out of the camera. I couldn't see a thing for a few seconds. Turning around towards me, Mom pushed a button and the light bulb would pop out and into my hands. I'd juggle it till it cooled off. Just another thing to put into my toy box.

It took two months to get the pictures back because they had to come all the way from America. The bear pictures were always the same. A blank picture with a round bright spot in the middle. I don't know how many times Mom tried to take a picture of a black bear through the window. But I do know that I never saw a bear in any of the pictures Mom took. Maybe Dad should have taken the pictures, he knows more about bears, 'specially when we go to the dump.

A piece of jam toast, a black bear, and a quiet hero at the wheel.

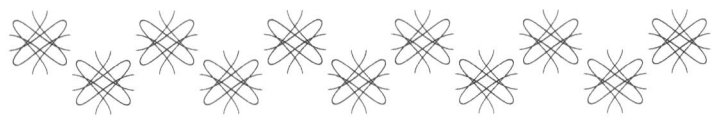

How I Learned to Love Clean Dirt

I've been three stupid days with a bad cold. I was sitting looking out our front window and watching Alaska Coastal planes land on the water in front of the Standard Oil Dock. I knew which airplanes were Grumman Goose or PPY. I liked the Grumman Goose the best. It was smaller and just looked cool. And they looked like they had bombs on the end of their wings.

Around eleven in the morning, I'd watch for Sam to head down the hill. Sam lived right below us and was cool. He had coal black hair, slicked into a shiny DA. But that wasn't the coolest part. He had a black leather jacket, black pants, black engineer boots, and black gloves. I wanted to look like Sam. Instead I looked like a lump of used tissues. I needed to be outside playing with the gang.

Mom said it was a good time to practice reading a book. I didn't feel like reading a book. I couldn't read that well. Yet, I liked the pictures if they were cowboys, Roy Rogers, or Lone Ranger.

Blister came into my bedroom. Not really a bedroom. More of a closet with a bed in it. But it was mine, so I called it my bedroom.

"Hey, little guy, you done playing sick? You need to get out of bed, get dressed, and go play. You'll feel better," Blister said.

"I want to, but Mom says I got to stay in bed till I drink her get-well glob first."

"Drink it. Then I'll show you how to never get sick again."

"Really. You know how to do that?" I asked.

"Oh, yea. Wayne showed me. One of the older gang members showed him. It works. You ever see your bother sick?"

"Nope."

"You ever see me sick?"

"Nope."

"Okay then. Hurry up while it's still nice outside. We can't do it when it's raining."

"Mom," I yelled. "I'll drink your icky stuff."

She brought in a glass of orange and green looking liquid.

"What's in it and how did you make it, Mom?" I'd had it before and almost threw up. I needed to know in case the doctor asked me why I was in the hospital.

"It's all good for you, honey, it will help you have a B.M." Mom was always talking about B.M. That's when you go poop. She talked about that more than she talked about birthdays.

"I slice onions, sprinkle a little sugar in between the slices, and put it on the coolest part of the oil stove. Then I add garlic. Let it sweat for two days, and voilà! It's ready to drink. Your Uncle John drank that all the time, and he never missed a day of fishing."

I drank it in one fast gulp. My eyes crossed. My tongue did a somersault. I lay back down while my stomach talked to my back bone. This is not going to stay in my stomach. I had to talk to it 'cause I wanted to go outside with Blister.

"Mom, can I get dressed and go outside for just a little while? Blister says she needs me to play. Please, please?"

"Fine. But if you start to sweat, you come right back in."

"Yes. Yes. Thanks, Mom."

I got dressed and went looking for Blister. There she was reading a book on the back porch. She was always reading a book. Guess that's why she wore glasses. I didn't want glasses, so I decided not to do that much reading.

"I'm ready to go, Blister."

We lived right at the base of Mt. Roberts. The trail started just a few feet from our back door. We hiked up two switchbacks, then left the trail, and climbed up to an old tree stump. It was one of our forts. When it rained.

"You got to promise you won't tell Mom about this or I can't show you. It's for Starr Hill Gang members only. We promise never to tell anyone, or we'll be thrown out of the Gang."

"Okay. I promise! I promise! Do we cut our wrists and put our blood together?"

"No, don't be so stupid. We're not in a cowboy movie. We need clean dirt."

"Clean dirt?"

"Not all dirt is clean, stupid. That's why we gotta dig."

She dug around the stump. My eyes were fixed on her the whole time. She brushed way some old rotten part of the stump and took a handful of the dirt and smelled it. Frowned. Tossed it. She looked like a dog burying its bone. She did it a bunch of times. Then she smelled one and smiled.

"This," she said, holding it under my nose, "is clean dirt."

Blister was right. It didn't stink. Kind of smelled sweet clean.

"Here's what we have to do. Go find some big leaves. Not skunk cabbage leaves. Gotta be tree leaves. You got that?"

"Ah-huh."

I came back with three big leaves. Grabbing a handful of clean dirt, she started pounding the dirt into a paddy that looked just like a hamburger without the bun. She then folded the leaf over the paddy. Handed it to me.

"Now eat it. The whole thing. Remember it's clean dirt and that's good for you. You'll never get sick again."

She was smiling. That worried me.

"How is eating dirt good for you? Mom's always telling us to take off our shoes because we'll get dirt over everything and that can get us sick."

"Mom's talking about dirty dirt. This is clean dirt. You have little modules in your body, and, if you don't feed them dirt once in a while, you will be sick all the time. It's something I learned in science class. I started eating clean dirt years ago and haven't had a cold ever. I promise you; this will work the rest of your life. When you get older, people will ask you why you never got sick. Then you can tell them because you ate clean dirt. Don't forget to tell them your sister, with the enlarged brain, told you about it."

I looked at the dirt pie. It looked like dirt. It smelled like dirt. Clean dirt. Is this a bad idea? Is a cold that bad? I wasn't sure I knew. Blister was a lot smarter than me and she never did anything bad. I looked up at the sky. Didn't know what I was looking at. Just the sky. My eyes came back to the clean dirt pie.

I took a bite without realizing what I was doing. Like I always said, I don't spend a lot of time thinking, I just do. Not bad. I ate the whole thing. Then Blister and I walked home.

The next morning, I was up at the crack of dawn. I had some crunching going on when I moved my mouth but I didn't care. I had eaten the sure cure. I needed to think of getting something special for Blister. She's always taking care of me.

Even when it tastes like dirt.

A few weeks later, a kid who just moved on to Starr Hill was playing in his yard sniffling and coughing and walking around with toilet paper stuffed up his nose. My brain remembered what Blister did for me.

"Is your name Joey?"

"Yeah, who are you?"

"My name is Johnny, and it looks like you got a bad cold. I can help you get rid of it if you want me to."

"I'd really like that. I hate getting sick. Is your dad a doctor?"

"Nope, but my sister Blister showed me how to get rid of a cold and never get one again. I haven't been sick for two weeks now. Want me to show you?

"Okay, but my mother doesn't want me to leave the yard. Says there could be bad people here. We came from California, and we don't trust anybody."

"Don't worry. I'm with the Starr Hill Gang. We help kids all the time. But we got to find some clean dirt, and I don't think there's any in your yard. Let's sneak over to the big water tank. There's some clean dirt there."

"Okay, but we can't be long."

I did just what Blister did. Smelled the dirt 'til it was clean. Then I got a leaf that was kind of brown, but it still had a lot of green on it. I packed the clean dirt into a paddy and wrapped the leaf around it.

He took a bite and gagged so hard that he coughed up something from last Thursday. Then he spit the rest out and ran home screaming for his mom.

I never saw Joey again. I heard his family moved back to California. Probably rained too much in Juneau for them.

Blister found out and made me promise never to practice medicine again. She said dirt cures were only for gang members, and I'd broken the sacred trust.

But still, I haven't been sick since. Not a sniffle.

So maybe Blister was right.

Or maybe I'm just full of clean dirt.

Some kids took vitamins.
I took a bite out of Mt. Roberts.

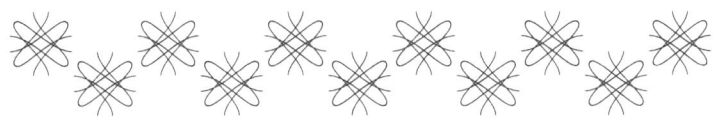

How I Gave Myself a Black "DA"

It was fall. Cold rain fell sideways like it always does when summer gives up.

Blister and I were down in the basement going through Dad's tools and jars of nails. Just junk. We didn't know what to do with any of it.

Blister grabbed a can of something. Had no label but it had some old black dried liquid going down the side of the can.

"What's that?" I asked.

"I don't know. It says creo... something. I don't know. Let's open it up and see."

Blister got a big screwdriver off Dad's work bench. She was really good with a screwdriver. She tried prying off the lid. It was stuck. She grabbed a big hammer off the work bench and hit the lid a couple of times. That put a big dent in it. She grabbed the screwdriver again. Gritting her teeth, she pried on the lid with all her might. The lid flew through the air landing on the floor. A black liquid stared back at us. We looked at each other. Smiling, Blister picked up the can and smelled it.

"Whew, it stinks. It don't smell like paint. You think creo... something is like paint? What do you want to do with it?" she asked.

I think I was born with a brain that doesn't think a lot about what's going to happen next. It just happens. Whoever gave me this brain might not have grabbed all of it off the shelf. Before I thought about anything at all. I grabbed the can and turned it over on top of my head.

The can stayed on my head like a helmet.

I laughed. "Lookie me! I got black hair just like Sam. I'm cool!"

Blister's eyes popped open. "Oh, no. Why did you do that. You're in trouble now and dumb too."

"No, I'm not. I'll just wash it off." I wasn't worried. Only girls get worried or scared. "It's ok. Wait for me, I'll be right back."

I ran upstairs and tried to sneak into the bathroom to wash the black liquid off my blond hair.

Mom walked into the kitchen and saw me sneaking. Black goo was dripping from my head like I'd combed my hair with tar.

"John, what have you got yourself into now?" Mom said.

Her eyes were blinking danger. Maybe anger.

"Oh, my goodness. What did you do? Did your sister pour that paint on you?"

"No, no. Blister didn't do a thing. Blister said it didn't smell like paint so it's probably not paint. It's okay Mom. I'll just wash it off and go back out and play."

Mom grabbed the kitchen chair, put it in front of the sink, then stacked some towels on the counter. Blue ones. My favorite color.

"Stand up on the chair. Don't move. Don't talk. And please don't think about anything!"

"CARLA, GET UP HERE NOW!" Mom yelled.

"What Mom," Blister said as she came through

the kitchen door. "I didn't do anything! Johnny just took that can and poured it on his head."

"Did you look to see if the can had any writing on it?"

"Ah, yea. I think it said something like CREO... But there was only part of a word."

Mom's face dropped. "Oh, no. It can't be creosote. There's nothing worse than creosote. I need your help and don't say a word. We have to get this off John's head now. Go down to the basement and get the turpentine. Run!"

I heard Blister run down the stairs. Then back up. She set the can on the counter with a big clunk.

"Mom, what's in that can?"

"It's turpentine. And I'm going to warn you. This is going to sting."

On no, not turpentine. Dad washed my hands with that once when I was helping him paint. He poured a little on my hands. It burned. It almost took the skin off my hands. Mom's not going to use that. Is she?

"Put your head over the sink and don't say a word. And whatever you do, don't open your eyes. Or your mouth. Remember you did this. You and that brain that does things without thinking there's going to be a tomorrow. This is the only way I know of to get that creosote off your noggin."

"Mom...maybe we could try some soap and water? Or maybe I could go down to the Evergreen bowl and go swimming. That water's already dirty so it won't matter."

She pushed my head down towards the bottom of the sink. I guess we weren't going to use any soap or water. Evergreen Bowl must be out too.

I heard the cap unscrew. The smell hit my nose. I stunk like gasoline that Dad put in the old car.

She held the can over my head and a little drippled out. Instant heat. She grabbed a towel and scrubbed. Then she did it again and again and again. I was wiggling doing a tap dance on the chair. I knew there wouldn't be any hair left on my head. It felt like Mom had built a bonfire on top of my head. I need to go out to the glacier and put my head in an iceberg.

"How you doing, honey?" Mom asked.

I couldn't open my mouth 'cause she said to keep it closed, so I just nodded and wiggled.

She yelled to Blister to bring more towels. She didn't sound happy. I think Blister made her mad.

It seemed like I had been standing there all day. I needed to go pee, but I couldn't open my mouth to tell her.

I could hear Mom and Blister talking in the living room. Something about "how stupid can you be." I knew Blister wasn't stupid 'cause she read all the time. Mom came back into the kitchen and poured more turpentine on my head. I couldn't feel anything anymore. Finally, she toweled me off and said to put my head under the sink faucet again.

"Carla, grab the Fels-naphtha soap from under the sink. Better grab the A-Jax too."

Mom turned on the water. Cold. Then grabbed the Fels-naphtha and started scrubbing my head again. Then she put down the Fel's-Naptha and picked up the can of A-Jax and sprinkled some on my head. I wanted to sneeze. I didn't. She rubbed it in with her hands. Then grabbed a brush and started really scrubbing. Hard. Now I knew you could probably see my thoughts through the top of my head. She rinsed my head with cold water. That felt cool. Dried off my head and told me to sit on the couch and not to move.

I'd still be sitting there, but Blister came in and said let's go build a fort. She was a good fort builder, and I didn't care about my head. It burned but, I'd seen cowboys have a lot bigger problems than I did. I remember John Wayne got shot once but kept on shooting.

Later that year, I saw Sam walking down Starr Hill probably heading to some bar. He still had that black DA. And still looked cool.

I waved and said, "Hey Sam! I tried out your hairstyle. Once."

He looked confused and kept walking. Probably didn't recognize me with that scab on my head.

I smiled. I didn't tell him it took two days, two gallons of turpentine, and all the skin off my scalp.

But for about ten glorious seconds…

I was cool!

I lost some skin, half my dignity, and maybe a layer of skull. But I looked sharp doing it!

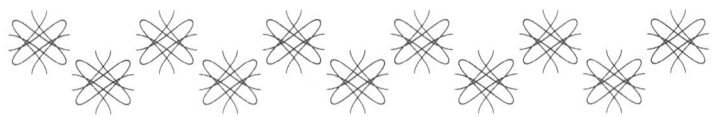

A Tinkle in His Eye

I sat on the potty. Not on the potty, but on the piece of wood that covers the potty. Because if I didn't, I'd fall in. I did that once. That's how I know.

I was waiting for Dad to come in and do his morning magic. I wanted to do something special for him. Something that would make me tinkle in his eye. But first I had to watch him, so I would know how to do it.

The door knob turned. In came Dad. Dressed in his morning whites. He had on his white baggy underpants and a white T-shirt. He didn't have on his long johns 'cause it was summer. He walked in and closed the door. He looked over at me and smiled. Dad didn't talk a lot. He left all that talking to my mommy and Blister.

He turned on the hot water faucet and then leaned over the sink—his head was almost in the sink—scooped up some hot water and splashed it onto his face. He stood up and shook the water off just like my dog Mike after a rain storm. Dad glanced my way, with a little grin. And blinked.

He opened the mirror door and reached inside of the hole in the wall and grabbed a big white coffee cup with waxy stuff in it. "Old Spice" was written on it. He set it on the sink. I couldn't read, but he told me that's what the cup said. Then he grabbed a round paint brush and put it on the sink. Finally, he grabbed a shiny silver hammer-looking thing he called a razor. I liked to call it the silver hammer.

He told me not to play with it 'cause it was sharper than a knife.

He turned on the hot water handle and a put a little tiny bit of hot water in the Old Spice cup. He grabbed the round paint brush that had a big round handle and started swirling the brush around the cup. Fast! Real fast. Magic happened. White foam started to grow. Like ice cream, without the cold. He looked at me and blinked again.

"I'm going to put a little spice in my life," he said.

He smeared that magic foam all over his face, just below his eyes. Not on his forehead. Not on his nose. Just the part where Dad grows furry.

He washed out the cup and brush and put them back in the hole in the wall. He shut the mirror and then picked up the silver hammer.

Starting by his right ear, he scraped the white stuff away, holding his chin with the other hand. I guess he thought it might run away or something. My dad's smart, but he just put that white stuff on and now he's already scraping it off. I thought that was stupid.

I know my mom would never be that dumb.

He'd lifted his chinny-chin-chin real high and scraped under it. He stretched his face out, so far his tongue almost fell out. I watched with big eyes. I needed to know every move for my plan to work.

Now came the part I didn't understand. And I didn't know how to do it either. I was standing on the potty watching with big eyes. He pushed his upper lip way out, all funny and long. Almost past his nose. He had a clown's face. He brought the razor slowly down from under his nose to his lip. Three times.

Dad leaned over the sink again, turned on the hot water, and washed all the foam off that he missed. Oh-oh, he had two spots where a little blood was seeping out from the inside of his head. He opened the medicine cabinet, took out a little bottle with a red cap that had a white stick in it. He took the stick out of the bottle and rubbed where the blood was oozing out. He reached past me and grabbed some potty paper. Patted the blood off his face. Taking a tiny piece of potty paper, he put it over the blood. Trying to hide the cut so Mom wouldn't know.

I only use potty paper for potty business. Dads can do whatever they want 'cause they're smart. Sometimes. But my mommy is too. I'd never seen potty paper on her face.

"Won't be long and you're going to have to do this every morning," Dad said, as he left me standing on the potty with my mouth wide open. All alone. In the bathroom, but ready to try it.

Saturday came. It was pouring so hard I knew the gang wouldn't want to play outside. Mom was ironing. She's always ironing. And Dad was at the old yellow wooden kitchen table smoking a Camel cigarette and trying to fix our toaster.

I didn't like Camels. I liked Lucky Strikes. They had the *Yours Truly, Johnny Dollar* radio show, and I could say, L.S.M.F.T., *Lucky Strikes*

Means Fine Tobacco." I could say it better than the announcer. But I like the Camels pack better. It had a big brown camel with one bump on his back. That bump was bigger than the mountain it was standing by.

I walked through Mom and Dad's bedroom, dragged a chair from the side of the bed, and pushed it into the bathroom. Closed the door, got up on the chair, and faced the mirror.

It was my time. I could feel my heart racing around in my shirt. Mom's and Dad's eyes would be sparkling with pride when I walked out with my face held high and showed them.

I remembered everything. I turned on the hot water and splashed some water on my face, then I shook it off. I pulled the mirror open. I had to get up on my tippy toes to reach inside the hole in wall to get the big white coffee cup. I got it down and set it on the sink. It was really heavy. Then I got the round paint brush and the silver hammer. I put a few drops of hot water in the Old Spice cup.

With the paint brush, I swirled, swirled, swirled. Ice cream magic. Not cold. Just creamy.

I stood tall on the chair. I breathed in a couple of deep breaths. My eyes sparkled. I had the look of an old man. "I gonna put a lot of spice in my life." I blinked.

I grabbed the shoe brush with white all over it and looked over at the empty potty seat. I blinked both my eyes. I smeared it all over my face. Getting some in my eyes. It burned. With my eyes closed, I found a towel and wiped all the white stuff off my face. I could see again. I started over. Carefully. Slowly. I set the paint brush down. I looked in the mirror. White stuff was in all the right places.

I picked up the silver hammer, held my chinny-chin-chin with my left hand. I slid the silver hammer down the right side of my face. No problem. I put the silver hammer under the hot water. Shook it. Then I put the silver hammer in my left hand and held my chinny-chin-chin with my right.

My left hand went zig-zagging to my ear. I pulled away. I tried again. This time it went to the top of my head. I set everything down on the sink. Dad didn't use his left hand. Just his right hand. I grabbed the silver hammer in my right hand, reaching across my nose, and holding my chinny-chin-chin with my left. I scraped down. It worked. I took another deep breath. I'm not gonna use my left hand ever again. Maybe to read with.

Now came time to do the major cutting. I opened my mouth and stuck my pointer finger in between my upper lip and my front teeth. I looked in the mirror. Same face as Dad's. Slowly I scraped down from under my nose to where my lip joined my mouth. My chest was starting to bulge out. I saw the start of a smile. Like Dad's. I did it again. One more time. Just as I was going to do it again, my bottom needed an itching. I moved my left hand down to scratch my bottom but I forgot to tell my right hand what I was doing.

SLICE.

A sharp sting flew to my brain. Blood began shooting out. My eyes were glued to the mirror. This is a lot bigger than Dad's cut. The blood didn't scare me because I was almost a man. Maybe a short man. A bleeding short man.

I grabbed the little bottle with the white stick in it. Just like Dad. I took the stick out. Just like Dad. Swiped it across the hole in my face. This wasn't like Dad's.

Ran out of the bathroom like a cat on fire. I screamed. Loud. Someone had ripped my face off. I ran into the living room where Mom and the ironing board were.

"Bert, oh hurry, Bert," Mom yelled. "Johnny has blood running down his face. Hurry."

Mom was shaking like a leaf in a wind storm.

Dad walked into the living room. He kneeled down, putting both of his hands on my shoulders. "Did you try shaving?" he asked with a smile.

"Uh huh."

"Did you use the styptic?"

"Huh?"

"Did you use the little white stick I use when I cut myself?"

"Uh huh."

He picked me up under his arm and carried me into the kitchen. I was getting blood all over him. And the floor. My screams had melted away. He put my head under the cold water. I could see the blood going around and round in a circle before it disappeared down the hole in the sink. The stinging slowly went away. The blood was slowing down too. I think I was running out.

Dad set me on the chair. "Don't move."

"I'm not going anywhere." *I don't think I have enough blood to go anywhere.*

Dad came back holding a band-aid. Grabbing the dish towel and wiping off my face, he put the band-aid on my cut and said, "Maybe we could wait another ten years before we try shaving again. Why don't you show your mom your band aid?"

I walked into the living room to show Mommy my band-aid, but she was walking around the ironing board saying something about she couldn't believe her little boy would do that. I don't know who she was talking to, so I decided I better go to my room.

I knew then, my dad was tough. He never cried or screamed when he put the white stick on his face.

But then again, he was my dad.

Now I had to find a new way to put a tinkle in my daddy's eye.

He didn't say much, just smiled and handed me a bandage.
That's how my dad said, "I love you."

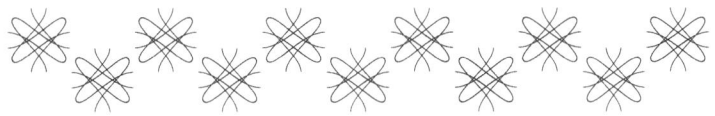

Catalog Kid

The Fifth Street Grade School was about to explode. Juneau's school system would never be the same. I be going into second grade with a brain the size of a grizzly bear's.

Mom gathered Blister, who was three years older than I was, into the living room along with me to order new clothes for school. It was the middle of summer, but things took a long time to come to Juneau. Everything came by boat...the Alaska Steamship Line. Lugnut, who was three years older than Blister, making him, ah, a lot older than me, had to get his clothes somewhere else. He wore giant clothes...probably from a garage. They were always greasy. And stunk.

On the floor were two big books. Sears and Roebuck and Montgomery Wards. I had already peeked through my favorite catalog and picked out the shirt I wanted. I had to tell Mom which ones would look good on me. As always, I had to be second. Blister was first. A stupid girl.

"You can sit here on the floor with us, but you have to be quiet and not squirm around. Or you can go over and pet Mike, he'd probably like that," Mom said.

"I'll sit right here 'cause Mike's wet and stinks like the garbage can."

Mom and Blister started flipping the pages on both big books like it was story time. They didn't care if they was looking at glasses, cooking junk, or camping junk. They thought all that junk belonged in our house. When they got to girl's clothing, they got more stupid.

"Oh, isn't that cute," flipping the page... "isn't that beautiful." Flip. "Wait...that's adorable."

That dumb skirt went from cute to beautiful in less time that it takes Mike to shake off the rain. I wouldn't wear any of them. This was stupid, and I was afraid my book would be out of my clothes by the time Mom got around to me.

Finally, after Blister had picked out enough clothes to open her own store, Mom had her stand on a piece of white paper on the floor. Then chased her foot around with a pencil. I'm giggling. Maybe they were getting her flippers. I didn't say a word. I needed that logging shirt.

Mom looked over at me. "Okay, John, let's order your clothes. Then I need for you to be in bed by 8:30. No squirming. Just do as I ask for once."

"Mom, can I show you the shirt I think will look good on me?" Turning to Page 264 of the Montgomery Ward's catalog, I plopped the book down in front of her pointing at that beautiful shirt. "That's it."

I had used my crayons to draw bright red and yellow lines around it. Wow! It stood out from all the rest. My shirt was red with little orange lines running through it, all in white squares. Jeepers. I be looking like a real logger. I held my breath, as my eyes begged Mom.

"Let's do your underwear first," she said. "Then we'll talk shirts."

"I don't need any underwear. I have four. All I need is a new shirt, Mom."

"Remember what I said. No horsing around. Let's look at your Montgomery Wards catalog. We don't need to look at both. Remember I want you in bed at 8:30. Look, it's already ten after eight."

Mom ordered my underpants, white. Undershirt, white. Socks, white. Long johns, white. All small. I think that's the only way they come.

I stood still and Mom put Dad's measuring tape around my waist. When she put it inside of my leg by my fly (Dad calls my zipper a fly), and I starting giggling.

"Stop that!"

I stopped.

Down the leg the tape went, wiggling like a worm. How dumb. I already knew my size. Small.

"Okay, let's look at the shirt you picked out."

Grabbing the catalog and opening to Page 264, I held my breath. I'm gonna get that cool logging shirt.

"Stand completely still and put your right arm out straight. That's fine, the left one will work." Smiling and shaking her head. She's always smiling when I do something right.

Mom turned the page to 265. My heart fell into my socks. These shirts were all one color. One color—how stupid is that! Loggers don't wear one color.

"No, no, Mom, it has to have lots of colors. Please, oh please. I'll be nice to Blister and keep my room clean!"

"Okay, one plaid flannel shirt."

Mom just giggled and wrote something down on a piece of paper. I knew she ordered the logging shirt.

"Okay, you saw Carla stand on that white piece of paper. I'd like you to do the same thing. And no playing around or that shirt will go to the Salvation Army."

Putting my hand into my mouth I looked at the ceiling. Mom kept chasing my foot around, and I kept putting my hand farther in my mouth.

"Why you chasing my foot, Mom?"

"I am going to send this in with the order. That way they will send you the right size boot. Go brush your teeth and skedaddle to bed. Thank you for being a brave boy and letting me trace around your foot. I know that was hard to be still for that long. But when you put your mind to it, you can do it."

All I care about is keeping Mom happy, so I'd get my logging shirt.

After a long time, a big box came with all our clothes in it. Mom told Blister and I to go try on everything. "Make sure they fit. If they don't, I'll have to ship them back right away."

"Mom, do I have to try on every one of those underpants? And every t-shirt? And every stupid sock?"

"No, just one of your t-shirts and one of your underpants. But the shirts and jeans you need to try on all of them."

I took all my clothes and set them neatly on the floor. I pulled out my shirt. My eyes lit up. Walking into Blister's room, I stood in front of the mirror and put on my shirt. For a second, I saw a short man with a red and orange logging shirt, steel helmet on his head, axe in hand. A real logger. Then I blinked. Logger John, gone. Just me and the mirror.

The shirt fit. I bet the orange shirt was the same color as my eyes. I went to try on the jeans. Oh, no. I almost started crying. Grabbing both pairs of jeans, I ran down to the basement. Dug around Dad's workbench. Found a hammer. Started beating like crazy on those jeans.

"JOHN HAROLD, WHAT ARE YOU DOING? STOP

RIGHT NOW!"

Mom used Harold. I was fried.

"Mom, they put pieces of wood where the knees are supposed to bend. The gang will laugh at me with baby padded knees. Only babies wear those stupid pants."

"It's not wood, and they're not baby jeans. They're reinforced so I don't have to patch them every month. Leave the knees alone and put that hammer back. Now go to your room."

With my head hanging down almost to the ground, I walked slowly back upstairs to my room. I can't wear these jeans to the fort? Or school? Everyone is gonna laugh. I don't care about holes. Everybody has holes in their jeans. Mom was ruining everything. Mom used to be fun.

I woke up to rain and wind. It didn't matter, and I didn't care. This is John's Day. First day of school, and I'll be wearing my logger shirt. I wanted suspenders and a steel hat but didn't ask. I hate hearing that word NO.

After I arrived at school, a nice lady showed me where to hang my coat. JOHN B in big letters was right above the hook. I hung up my coat. As I walked into the Miss Aamot's classroom, my chest was sticking way out. I bet you could see my chest bones poking through my red, orange, and white logger shirt. I stopped. Water filled my eyes. My stomach wanting to come up and join the floor. I didn't like school anymore.

All the boys in the classroom were staring at me. Half of them were wearing my shirt. Some in red and orange with white squares...my shirt. Some had stupid blue and green with white squares on their shirts. All of them. Plaid.

I was ready to explode. How could my Mother do

that? How could she tell all those other Moms what shirt I picked out?

I looked down at my chest. It was still sticking out, but now if felt more like a balloon that someone let the air out of.

The shirt wasn't special. A plaid, second-grade, betrayal uniform.

I slumped down in my seat, crossed my arms and closed my eyes. I could feel the heat rising on my neck.

That's when Miss Aamot walked over. Smiled really big. She said loud enough for everyone to hear, "Well, don't you boys look adorable! Like a little men's lumberjack club!"

I looked down at my desk and thought that maybe I should've worn those baby jeans. At least no one had any of them.

Never trusting a catalog or my mom again.

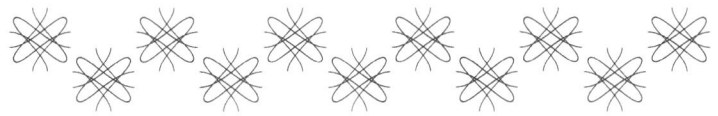

Why Alaska isn't in America

My third-grade teacher is one person I'll never forget. Not just because she taught us stuff like how to spell February or why we had to memorize the times tables...but because every morning around ten, she'd let us go outside and play. We have lunch at twelve. Then at two, she let us out to play again. That was really nice of her.

One day, Miss Murphy was talking about the time when America bought Alaska from Russia for 7.2 million dollars. That was a lot of money. I don't even know what a million dollars looks like, let alone seven. But why the two cents?

I raised my hand.

She took her time, figuring I was raising my hand to go to the little boy's room. I did that all the time but this time I didn't need to go.

She finally gave up. "Yes, John."

"Miss Murphy, I don't think Alaska is part of America," I said.

She gave me one of those teachers' looks. "John, why would you say that?"

"Well," I said, "on the back of my Checker Wheats box, there's a place where you can order a submarine. If you put baking soda in it, it goes down under the water and comes back up. Hopefully. It sounds so neat. I'd love to have one. But it says it takes four box tops and twenty-five cents. Which I don't understand 'cause my box of cereal only has one box top. Not four."

"John, why don't you explain to the class what you meant by Alaska not belonging to America," she said with a trying grin.

"I'll try. At the bottom of the box it says, 'Offer only valid in the Continental United States' and, "not Alaska and not Hawaii. So I guess we're not part of America."

She stared at me. "John…I don't believe that's what it means."

"In fact," I said. "Alaska is not even on the same continent as USA. Maybe it's an island like Hawaii. They say they don't allow islands. That's what it says. Honestly. Right there on the bottom of the box. I'm not making this up, Miss Murphy."

She rolled her eyes. Backwards. "You might want to consider becoming a lawyer someday."

That confused me.

The box didn't say anything about being a lawyer… all I got out of the box was some crunchy brown dried up sticks that tasted just like the sawdust on the floor of the meat market where my dad worked. That stuff was yucky. I hated it. But the box had great toys if only I could get them. But, they didn't believe Alaska and Hawaii were in America. And Miss Murphy didn't know that.

Maybe I should be the teacher.

When Miss Murphy went out of the room, Ruth and Karen, who sat next to me, came over and stood at my desk. Wagging their finger.

"You shouldn't argue with Miss Murphy," Ruth said.

"Yea, and she's a lot smarter than you too," Karen added.

What do girls know? They probably don't even know what a submarine is. And I wasn't arguing with Miss Murphy. I just wanted her to know that she didn't know Alaska wasn't part of America, but that I knew it.

Girls!! I decided I'd get even with those girls at recess.

At ten o'clock, we went out behind the school and lined up to play red rover. Doc, my best friend, stood beside me. Finally, the call came.

"Red rover, red rover, send Johnny right over."

"Go, Johnny. Show them girls who you really are," Doc said.

I looked for Ruth and Karen. Good. They were standing together in the line. Holding hands. Their lips and hands squeezed so tight that they were turning white. They knew I was coming for them. I bet they wished they hadn't waved their fingers at me. I lowered my head, ran towards their hands like a bowling ball on its way to the pins.

I wasn't big. I wasn't fast. But I was always ready. My speed was slightly more than a speeding turtle. About one mile an hour when I exploded into their arms. I bounced off. Everything turned upside down. I was on my back, looking up at them. Karen and Ruth looked down. Smiling.

They both blurted out. "Would you like to join us girls, Johnny?"

Gee-whiz! In America I bet the girls aren't as tough playing Red Rover as the girls in Alaska. In Alaska, they knock you flat on your back.

Doc helped me up. Patted my back.

"Next time," he said. "Aim for someone smaller."

"Yeah, or maybe I'll just collect four box tops and move to the Continent."

I questioned America and got flattened by girls.

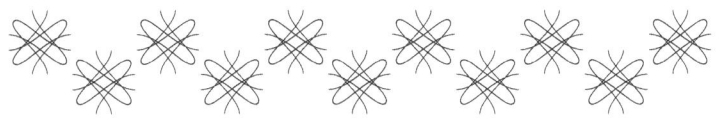

Buying Muscle

Dad and I were sitting at the old yellow wooden kitchen table. I was staring at a pile of smashed-up grass on my plate that somebody tried to pass off as food. It didn't belong in my mouth. It didn't belong anywhere. It belonged back in the yard.

"Dad," I said, stabbing it with my fork. "I need some muscle. Okay? I really need to get some big muscles. Everyone has muscles except me. And Mike. He doesn't need any, he's a dog. But I need them bad."

"You can start by eating that spinach on your plate. Look what it did for Popeye. Let's eat up. If you eat your spinach, I'll show you something special."

I took my fork and pushed the pile around. It didn't disappear. I pinched my nose shut and shoveled the pile into my mouth. It fell onto my tongue, then slithered down my throat to my tummy. It felt alive like a green frog. My stomach yelled back. "What did I ever do to you?"

"Dad, in the back of my comic book *Casper the Friendly Ghost* there is a place where you can order muscles. For real. I'd like to get some. I mean a lot!"

"Order muscles?"

"Yeah! You just send them money, and they

will send you a special book. There's a picture of a skinny guy walking down a beach and this big guy with really big muscle, kicks sand on him. That wasn't nice. Then this mean guy calls him a sissy. So skinny goes home, picks up his comic book and orders his special muscles. And boom! He turns into a guy with muscle everywhere. He has them in his arms, his legs, and even a bunch in his neck... um. I don't want them in my neck. How can I turn my head? I only wanted them where Popeye had his. Arms."

"And how much do these muscles cost?" Dad asked, with his usual smile.

"Oh, I'm not sure. But if you loan me a dollar, I could find out."

"How about you find out without the dollar. You know, you don't buy muscles. You build them. Let me show you something."

Dad still had on his white shirt from the meat market where he worked. He unbuttoned his white shirt and hung it on the kitchen chair. I stared at his arms. They were big. Not as big as Popeyes. Nothing that looked like a can of spinach would explode out of.

"What you gonna do, Dad?"

"Just sit and watch. You don't need money to build muscle. Just hard work."

He planted his right elbow on the table. Then he stuck his right thumb in his mouth. He started to blow into his thumb like he was filling a balloon. His cheeks slowly grew...bigger, really big. Like they were gonna explode. All at once a hissing sound came out of his mouth. With his left hand, he pointed to his muscle right above his Popeye muscle.

My eyes stared at it. The hissing kept hissing. His muscle right above his Popeye muscle started to move. Up. Oh, my golly. It was getting bigger. And bigger. So were my eyes. I'd never seen Dad's muscle so big. How big can his muscle get? He had a lot more muscle than Old Skinny and maybe that mean guy too that were in the back of Casper the Friendly Ghost comic.

I slid off my chair. Walked around the table. Took my finger and poked his muscle. It felt like our garbage can. I went to poke it again, but Dad pulled his thumb out of his mouth and it quit hissing. There was one last fizz sound like a soda going flat. Then it just disappeared. Gone. I stood there looking, staring.

"See, you don't need to go buy muscles. All you have to do is work hard, and they will build themselves. I could line up some jobs for you that will help you to start building those muscles."

"Yea, but if I just buy them then I don't have to work. Then I could play. I've got a new fort to build."

Dad just smiled.

"Hey Dad," I said. "What if I blow really hard and maybe I could get one that way. Let me try it Dad? Please."

"Okay, but you need to have some muscle to blow up before it will work."

"Does it matter what thumb I blow into?"

"No, go ahead, give it a try," he chuckled.

I took off my shirt. It had all the orange and white squares on it. Then I hung it neatly on the floor. I didn't have a t-shirt on so I sat there with no shirt at all. I was shaking a little 'cause the room was cold. I put my right elbow on the table. Stuck my left thumb in my mouth.

"No, no," Dad said, "the other thumb, Johnny. You're blowing into the wrong thumb. You need to blow into the one that's connected to the elbows that's on the table. Just blow as hard as you can."

He was wiping his eyes. I guess I was making him proud. He had a real big smile.

I shoved my right thumb into my mouth. Began blowing. My stomach slowly started to grow. I wondered if my cheeks were growing too. I couldn't see 'em. I thought I could see them out the bottom of my eyes. But, my muscle that should have popped up, stayed where it always stayed. Hidden.

"See, Dad, I gotta order those muscles or the big kids will be kicking sand on me. You and Mom don't want that. So, let's order them tonight. Then, I promise I'll be good all the time. What do you say Dad? Please?"

"Let me sleep on it for a couple of days."

"That's a long time to sleep."

I went to my room and put my thumb in my mouth. The right one this time. I was going to show Dad I could do it. I'd practice 'til he woke up. I still thought it would be easier to just buy muscles.

Muscles were gonna take a long time. But at least I didn't have to eat any more spinach.

Turns out, real muscles take longer and taste like spinach.

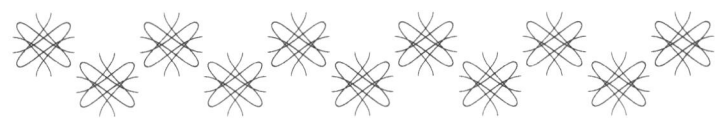

Bottom Burp

"Mommy, Mommy, Daddy gave me a bottom burp!"

Mom turned from the stove, holding a spaghetti covered spoon. "Your Dad did what?" Mom asks.

"All I was doing was playing with Mike on the floor and Daddy said, "Come pull my finger." So, I jumped up and ran over and pulled Dad's finger. Not the short one he cut off with the hamburger saw. The one right next to it. You know, the one he points with to tell me to go to bed. Then BOOM! It was loud. Really loud, Mom. I never heard Dad be so loud before."

Mom wiped tears from her eyes with the corner of her apron.

"What did you call it, and where did you hear that before? A bottom burp?"

"Yeah! Grandma B said in England, where she lived when she was little, that's what you call it when gas comes out your back end. Is that okay to say?"

"Yes. Yes, you can say that but, I'm going to have a talk with your Father."

Ran back into the living room waving my arms like I was landing a plane.

"Daddy, Daddy, I think you're in trouble. Mom wants to talk to you while Mike and I play. I didn't say anything wrong. I promise."

"What do you need, Honey?" Dad asks, walking into the kitchen.

"Bert," Mom said, pointing her spaghetti spoon at him like it was a sword. "I spend all day trying to teach these kids some manners, and you walk in and blow it...literally. In five seconds. Can you please refrain from having the children pull your finger? Especially John. Please."

"I'll work on it. Now I'm going to change my clothes and listen quietly to the radio. Without anyone talking," Dad said as he walked by me. Frowning.

The next night I'm waiting by the door for Dad to come home. It's our time. Dad and I could do something together. He's always working, or I'm always building forts so we never have any time together. But this was something we could do together. All by ourselves.

"Dad," I said as he hung up his coat. "I'd like you to have another bottom burp. If I have to pull your finger to make it work, I'll do it. So, let's go in the living room. Okay Dad. Let's do it together. Please! It'll be our time together."

Dad never had been a talker. He always smiles and goes about what he is doing when I ask him questions.

"Let me go kiss your Mother. Then I'll meet you in the living room."

Oh boy, I'm gonna hear a bottom burp, and I'm the one that's gonna make it work. Yippee! I can hardly wait 'til I show Blister the magic Dad and I can do.

"Come on, Dad. Kiss Mom. Let's do it."

Dad had on his white shirt, that's what a meat man always wears. And brown pants. He doesn't have any blood on his shirt or pants. He usually does. Ugh.

"Which finger do you want to pull?" Dad asks.

Hmm, which finger. If I pull the same one as I did last night, I'll hear the same thing. A loud boom. Maybe I should pull the one that's been cut off. The short one. Maybe a little boom will come out. I don't know.

"Hurry up, I want to go change my clothes and listen to the radio before we eat. You said you want to do it right now, so let's do it."

"Okay. Dad can I pull two fingers? Just to hear if they're different. That okay isn't it?"

"Just pull one tonight and maybe tomorrow we can do both. Let's go!"

Dad puts his hand out like he's going to shake hands. I stare. I close my eyes and reach for his short finger. That's all I need. I pulled.

BOOM! I can't believe it. I made Dad's bottom burp. It wasn't as loud. I needed to learn how to do this. I haven't had much luck blowing up my Popeye muscle, but this looks a lot easier. I'm going to do this 'til I can show Blister. She'll be proud of me.

"Bert!" Mom's voice fills the room. Louder than the bottom burp. Bet Dad's in trouble. I dove behind the couch.

After two weeks of thinking and grunting, it was time to show Blister. She walked in and set her books on the kitchen table and looked at me.

"Hey, Blister, I got something to show you. Bet you never seen this before."

"What is it? I have to get my homework done so I can listen to Johnny Dollar tonight. Or did you forget?" Blister said. "Hurry up."

"It won't take a second. Come over and stand by me."

Blister sighed and stood in front of me. She was taller, older, and bossier.

But I was smarter.

"Now what?"

I stuck out my finger. The one I always point with. "Pull my finger!"

"No, I don't want to hear you fart. Did Dad pull that on you?"

"Yes, you too?"

"Yes, I'm going to my room to study. If you had a brain you might try it."

"Please, just once. I want to see if I can do it. It won't take a second and then you can go. I want to show the gang, but I have to test it first."

Blister rolled her eyes, grabbed my finger, and yanked. I tighten every muscle I owned. Belly, back, eyebrows. My face puffed up like a balloon animal. I held my breath. Pushed. Pushed harder.

I felt movement. My eyes are trying to bulge out of my head. Fuzzy. I can't see that well. Oh-no.

"What are you doing? Your face is all red. Breathe! Breathe Johnny."

Too late! I ran for the bathroom like I was chasing a bus. This isn't a bottom burp. This is the real thing.

Blister goes running into the kitchen laughing, "John pooped his pants. Ha ha. Mom, Johnny pooped his pants. Can we put him in a cage?"

I sat on the toilet, pants at my ankles. Wondering where my life had gone wrong. Then I heard footsteps.

The door cracked open just enough for Dad to peek in. He didn't say anything at first. Just smiled.

Then he whispered. "Wrong muscle, son."

He closed the door. Still my hero.

But I was gonna wait a long time before pulling anyone's finger again.

*Turns out, timing isn't everything
...but muscle control is.*

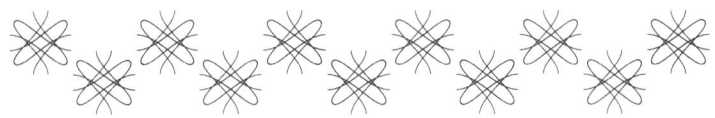

Chocolate Fort

Mom and Blister left me home all alone as they headed down to Harry Race Drug Store to pick up some medicine. I heard something about horse pills. I bet they're for Blister.

I waited until the door clicked shut. Then I stood in front of the refrigerator. My dreams were about to come true.

Our refrigerator is taller than me. And Blister. But Lugnut's bigger. He can even see what's on the top of the fridge. It's all white, except for the ketchup I left on the door handle. It makes a lot of noise like there's mice or somebody running around inside it. But it's ours.

Mom didn't know I had been watching her after she gave Blister and me that one square of candy. I followed her like a cat in the night. She wrapped the candy in silver paper then hid it up in the icebox behind the sour cream that no one ever touched.

"Just one piece each night," she said.

There were a lot more squares left on the bar. I didn't want them to go bad, so I needed to put a few, maybe four, in my tummy. I need to hurry before they come back home.

But I knew where the chocolate was sitting. Cold and all alone. It could go bad. I should save it.

I pushed the kitchen chair to the icebox and climbed up. The icebox door had ice on it, just like my bedroom window in the winter. After taking the candy bar...a Hershey, my favorite one, I climbed down and unwrapped the silver paper.

There were four squares across—and hold on—another four under that, and three more below. Wait. 1-2-3-4...and then 1-2-3-4 more...and then 1-2-3. My brain started to melt. I was no good at math. Especially when I was in a hurry. I had to count slow. 1-2-3-4. There, that made sense.

That was easy. My mind was racing. How many do I take without my mom knowing I borrowed some? If I took three, then she'd know, 'cause that's a uneven number and it made the candy bar uneven. I needed to take four. Or, what's four then another four? A lot. She'll never know. Those are even numbers. I counted out four, then another four and broke them off the bar. Wrapping the candy bar back up, I stuck it back in the icebox just like nothing ever happened. I climbed down off the chair, and my stomach started to gurgle. It knew what I had in my hand.

I sat down in front of the living room window. That way I could see when Mom and Blister were walking back up Starr Hill toward the house. I built a chocolate fort out of the chocolate squares on the table. I pretended the fort was on fire and started saving the citizens by eating them. One piece at a time. I had to move fast...the invaders (Mom and Blister) were on their way home.

I looked out the window. No Mom or Blister in sight. Safe for a while.

I kept playing. Now I only had two citizens left. I checked the window again. Mom and Blister were in front of Nancy and Buddy's house. They were only a block away. I had to save those last citizens. I shoved the last two pieces in my mouth. I wiped my face off on my sleeve. I jumped down and gathered up some comics books and pretended I was reading. I love to pretend. My favorite comic was *Roy Rogers*. Trigger would be proud.

"Honey, we're home. Did you take a nap when we were gone?" Mom asked.

Mom and Blister walked into the living room with a couple of bags that they set on the table. Mom looked at the table. Then at me.

"Come here," her friendly voice had changed.

I wasn't worried, she hadn't opened the ice box yet so she didn't know. I bet I did something else wrong. I walked over to Mom and smiled.

"What have you gotten into?

"Nothin'."

"What's that dark stuff all over your mouth? And what did you get on the table?"

I thought I wiped my mouth with my shirt. What went wrong?

"Oh, that. I might have had a piece of chocolate. Just one. And it was a small one. I didn't want to eat 'em all 'cause some belong to Blister. Sorry, Mom. I meant Carla."

"And where did you get the one small piece of candy?" Mom asked.

"I opened the fridge and there it was. I couldn't let it go to waste. So, I ate it. I really just borrowed it."

"You stole a piece of candy. How many did you take? Weren't you thinking about your sister at all? That's her candy too."

"Mom, I thought about Blister for a while, but she wasn't here. I didn't steal. I borrowed. I'll put it back if you give me some money so I can go buy another one."

"You go up to your room. There'll be no more candy. Your sister can have a piece of the Hershey bar tonight. Then I think it's time we stop having treats. I want you to think about the word STEAL. When you come back down you, will explain why you stole a piece of candy. Understand? Now skedaddle."

How am I supposed to tell her I stole when I don't know what it means? I know what steal means and no way did I steal. I borrowed. Dad would go next door to Fred's and borrow nails and pound them in a board. He didn't give the nails back. I did the same thing. Wonder if Mom got mad at Dad.

I needed to know if Mom looked in the fridge. I quietly opened my bedroom door. It squeaked. It always squeaks. Got down on my tummy by the stairs. Put my ear so I could hear down the stairs. I made sure my mouth was closed, 'cause Dad always said I could hear better if I kept my mouth closed. I listened. And listened. Oh no!! The refrigerator door closed.

"JOHN HAROLD, get down here. Now!"

I froze. I think my chocolate fort just collapsed in my tummy.

Didn't feel like stealing, 'til I got caught.

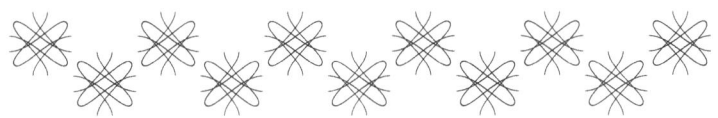

Purple Volcano

My mom was the best of Moms, but she had some far-out ideas. She'd read the *Look Magazine*, the Life Magazine, and *Reader's Digest* like they were cookbooks. Always looking for things to cook or projects for us kids. That's where her brain got scrambled. Blister and me would whisper, "What's she gonna do tonight—make us eat bear ears so we'll listen better?" Then we'd laugh.

One time, we were having dinner, maybe I was eight or seven, she came up with what she called a "Classy European Custom." She put this big bottle of purple stuff on the table. She called it "Mogen David." Then she put some little itty-bitty tiny glasses in front of each of us that my Lugnut called "Shot glasses,".

I figured that meant you shoot a big glass and whatever's left is the shot glass. Grownups are so stupid.

Mom poured a teeny bit of Mogen David wine–WINE!—into those tiny glasses and told us to sip it before dinner. She said it would help us "appreciate our food."

I didn't know what appreciate meant yet, but I knew I already loved food. In fact, I didn't need appreciate, I needed a bigger spoon.

That purple wine smelled and tasted like someone soaked their old wet socks in Dad's paint thinner, and then stored them for a thousand years and put it in a bottle. Since we never got much pop I thought. "Boy this is good."

One Friday night it was just me and Mom at home. Dad was pulling an overnight shift at the firehall. Volunteers do that. It was winter, so they drove around looking for chimney fires.

Blister was at her friend Pat's house. Lugnut was out looking for stupid girls. Or something. Mom and I had our shot glass of Mogen David, then we had hamburgers. I put ketchup and mustard all over mine. Just like the loggers do.

Mom lay down in her bedroom and put a wash cloth over her face 'cause she had one of her famous headaches. She always had one. Blister and Lugnut said they knew why, but wouldn't tell me.

Before Mom went to bed, she mumbled something about I should practice my reading. But *Yours Truly, Johnny Dollar* was on the radio. You can't practice when Johnny Dollar's solving somebody's murder. It's against the rules. Besides he's my favorite detective, and I'm gonna be just like him. But with a real gun. Or maybe a soldier. Maybe even a garbage truck driver. I knew I was gonna be somebody.

Then...I burped. Small one. I didn't spill any. It tasted like rotten grape jelly and those old wet socks. And it wouldn't go away. My brain told me the only way to fix a grape burp was to have more grapes.

I could hear my mom snoring. I knew the coast was clear. I tiptoed into the kitchen. Dragged a chair to the counter and climbed up like I was scaling Mt. Roberts mountain. I wrestled that giant jug of Mogen David down from the top shelf. Took both hands and all my strength, which at that point was about equal to a damp washcloth.

I didn't mess around with those stupid shot glasses. I poured myself a real glass of purple. I gulped it down. Wiped my arm across my mouth and gave nice big sigh.

It tasted the same. Dry and fuzzy. But now it made my tongue tingle. Like when I hit my elbow the wrong way. Dad called it a funny bone. Maybe I had a funny tongue. It felt loose in my mouth.

I got down. Rinsed the glass. Snuck into the bathroom and brushed my teeth 'cause Dad also said Mom could hear or smell a mosquito fart. That's what he said. After I was done, I sat down to think. By the radio.

My brain started thinking fast. Every time it raced, I'd get up on the chair and pour some more purple out. I think two, maybe three times. The jug was getting lighter and I got wobblier.

The burps were getting bigger, longer, and smellier. And they brought friends.

Every time I tried putting the jug back, it got heavier even though it was lighter. My legs turned to spaghetti. My eyes did cartwheels. And the stupid floor kept wanting me to join it. I needed to get low to the ground. Fast.

Lucky for me, my brain was still working. I now knew what appreciate meant. I appreciated the floor. I grabbed Dad's favorite lamp and took off the lamp shade. I stuck it on my head just like a soldier would do. I always wanted to be a sergeant in the Army. Tonight, that's what I was gonna be—Sergeant Bertholl. I sighed, and pushed my fallen chest out.

I walked out to the back porch and grabbed a broom. That was my rifle. Put it on my shoulder and started marching.

Just then *Fibber McGee and Molly* came on the

radio. I didn't understand what they were saying, 'cause they talked funny. So, I laughed and laughed 'til my belly was jumping up and down. It was just like when we told jokes at the fort. Laughing and slapping our knees.

I went back to marching in my underpants and t-shirt. Lampshade helmet bouncing on "me head," I was giggling like a crazy soldier. My rifle broom on my shoulder. When I passed by the big living room window, I saluted. Another soldier on the other side of the window saluted back.

I did an about face and walked in front of the window again. Saluted. "At ease, soldier." I heard that at the movies once. But that soldier saluted back. I saluted. He saluted.

"Stop saluting!" I saluted and he saluted. "STOP! STOP!"

Then the floor moved. It tilted. First right. Then left. I didn't know what was happening but it was happening.

"JOHN HAROLD, what in the world are you doing?"

It wasn't Fibber. Or Molly. It was Mom.

I froze in mid-salute. "I'm playing soldier, but this stupid soldier in the window won't stop saluting when I told him to. And, um...I got to tell you something, Mom."

She raised one eyebrow.

"I accidentally snuck a glass of purple wine. Just one. I think. I didn't mean to. But it was so good. I won't do that again, I promise."

I took off my helmet. Passed it and my gun to Mom. Then the floor gave out, and I was sitting on my bottom looking—I don't know, just looking. It felt like my stomach was looking too.

Mom shook her head, "I'm going put you in my

bed 'til you feel better. We'll talk about this in the morning."

Mom always has good ideas. Almost always. This was a bad, really bad one. As soon as my head hit the pillow, the ceiling started to spin. Slowly. Then faster, faster. Real fast. Then the walls started going around. But in a different direction. I grabbed the blankets and sheet. Holding on to them so I wouldn't be thrown through the window. One eye would open and the other would close. I couldn't control them.

Mom walked back into her bedroom. Took one look at me. "Are you okay, honey?"

I tried to say something, but my tongue had a pair of pajamas on it. Wool.

"MOMMM! WHOOOOOSH."

It happened!

The great purple volcano. A burp...gone rogue. Purple came out fast like a fire hose. Mom's walls, purple. Mom's sheets, purple. Mom's blankets, purple. Little Johnny, purple. Everything purple.

Except Mom's face. Red. Flashing red. Like the red light on the big fire truck that Dad drives.

Mom put me in the bath tub. Then tucked me into my bed.

When I woke up the next morning. I didn't feel very well. Mom was standing over me.

"What did you learn from last night?"

"That Mogen David wine don't appreciate me."

Even brave soldiers fall
...especially after three purple burps.

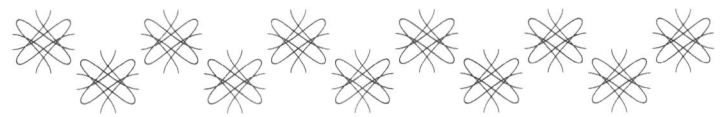

Shore Patrol

I gobbled down my hamburger like a starved grizzly bear. "Hey Mom, I gotta go meet Bingo and Bones. Okay?"

"Yes," she said, pointing her fork at me. "But I want you in by nine o'clock, not ten. I don't want to send Wayne out looking for you. Got that?"

"Yeah, see ya. Thanks for the hamburger, Mom," I yelled as I flew off the chair.

I raced down Starr Hill to chicken yard, where Bingo and Bones were waiting. We were all hyped up. Two big Navy ships in town and that meant one thing. Fights. The best place to watch them were the bars on South Franklin Street. There would be lots of fights. Guess they don't have anything to do on those big boats.

We hurried down Franklin Street 'til we got to Front Street. Wasn't much happening 'cause it was only seven pm. Lots of people just walking around talking. Sailors talking with high school girls.

I spotted the Basin Road Gang hogging the best seats on the wooden sidewalk in front of the Arctic Bar. The sidewalk was raised up like a stage. That's where the real action happened.

"Let's go check out the Top Hat Bar," I said. "Maybe Hattie's playing the piano."

When it's nice out, she'd push her big piano out onto the boardwalk and play. I've sat on her piano bench while she's played. I felt like I was playing. She's really nice. She calls it Honky-Tonk. It makes you want to get up and dance. I don't know how, so I just clapped my hands together and moved my head with the music. It's raining so we stand by the door and listen.

Across the street are the New York Tavern and Papa Ray's bar. Then a couple of stores down is Red Dog Saloon, the Arctic Bar, the Triangle Club and around the corner is the Imperial Bar. Oh yea, there's the Alaskan Bar, which is on the same side of the street as Hattie's. Bars lined both sides of the street all the way down to the City Café, but this is where all the fighting take place.

"Hey, the Basin Road Gang just left. Let's go grab their spot. It's the best spot in town," Bingo said.

"Let's go," Bones replied. "Hurry!"

We charged across the street and ran smack into two giants in Navy uniforms. Their white hats looked like crumbled up pancakes, and both had fat white bands around their arms with the big black letters "SP."

I looked up. "Mister, what's SP mean?" I asked.

The tall one bent down and looked me in the eye. "Shore Patrol. We're like the police but we travel with the ships. You thinking about joining the Navy. It's a lot of fun, and you see a lot of different places."

"Nope, I'm going be a paratrooper. I want to jump out of a plane. You ever jumped out of a plane, mister SP?"

"Ha, ha, we like being on the water. You could get hurt jumping out a perfectly good airplane. You guys be careful. It's going to get a little rough in a couple hours, and I'd hate to see you end up with fewer teeth than you started with."

"Thanks, we'll just hang out in doorways. We know how to stay…"

Just then a sailor came flying out of the Arctic Bar and landed on his back. Another navy guy flew out the door like a monkey and jumped on top of him and swinging his fist into his face. Fists flew. Blood flew. Spit flew.

Then the SPs took out their long, black billy clubs and started swinging them like they were conducting an orchestra of violence.

"There must have been a million of them fighting," Bones yelled.

We were jumping up and down yelling "HIT 'EM! HIT 'EM!" We were like cheerleaders.

More SPs came running, knocking people over the head. Sailors bleeding and screaming. This was more exciting than a stupid movie.

Two Juneau police cars with sirens blaring stopped in front of us. The police grabbed the sailors and threw them into the paddy wagon. It seemed like an hour or more before it was over. We were getting hoarse from all the yelling.

We decided to wander down to the New York Tavern.

"Hey!" Bingo shouted, "Look, it's someone's tooth."

He pointed to someone's front tooth lying on the sideway. Still bloody.

"Should we save it?" he asked.

"No way," I said. "We don't know whose mouth it's been in. Plus, sailors have backup teeth. Let's go so we don't miss any fights."

We saw five—maybe eight—more fights. None of them as good as the first one. John Wayne should have been in that one. It was a real fight. Blood, spit, torn shirts, yelling. It had it all.

I tapped another Shore Patrol guy on the elbow.

"Excuse me mister SP, do you know what time it is?"

"Yes, it's 2105."

"Is that SP time? We need Juneau time."

He and his buddy laughed. "Sorry, I thought you were in the Navy. It's 9:05 civilian time. You boys better head home because it's about to get worse."

"Thanks sir. We're headed home right now."

We nodded like good little civilians.

"Hey Johnny, you think you want to join the Navy?" Bingo asked as we walked back toward our houses. "You get to go all over the world. I've only been to the dump and out the road."

"I know I don't want to," Bones said, "You might get to go to a lot of places. But if they keep hitting you on the head with those billy clubs, you gonna have a headache all the time. Not me."

"How about it, Johnny?"

"Nah, I'm gonna join the Army like Audie Murphy. I want to jump out of airplanes. Ships are just giant fishing boats, and I get bored on ours. I gotta go. I'm five minutes late. My mom is going to kill me."

It was the best night of the week.

And I didn't even get hit.

*Not all boys go to war,
some just go downtown.*

Firefighters of Starr Hill

Most of us were eight or nine—or maybe seven. Some might've been something in between. A few of our dads belonged to the Juneau Volunteer Fire Department. Being proud sons, we decided to form our own. Thus, the Starr Hill Volunteer Fire Department was formed and led by the Starr Hill Gang.

Our fire truck was a go-kart that Lugnut had built years ago. It was more like a couple two-by-fours nailed together with an old piece of plywood on top. Two axles. Four wheels. And a patented sole brake system for stopping. Not top of the line. But good enough for the Starr Hill Gang.

Our biggest problem was the front axle—it always broke. Right in the middle. We'd take it down to a really nice man named Mr. Burrows, who was building a boat behind Juneau Motors. A huge boat. Out of iron.

"Mr. Burrows, we have a small problem, again," I said. "Our axle broke in the middle. Right where we want to put a big bolt through it so we can steer. Can you fix it again? Please? We don't have any money, but we think Buddy said he'd do some work for you," I said.

Mr. Burrows took the axle, squinted, and sighed. "Let me take a look. I don't know if there's enough metal left to weld, but I'll try. I don't take wooden nickels, but thank Buddy. I don't need him. Last time he swept the same pile of sawdust for over an hour."

He disappeared into his shop. We weren't allowed in there. I don't know why—we wouldn't steal anything. Then we saw the bright flashes and heard hammering. That meant he was working. A few minutes later, he came out holding our axle.

He stuck the axle in a big barrel of water. It must have been really hot 'cause steam came out rolling out. He took off his glove and felt it with his hand to make sure it wasn't hot and handed it to Bingo. He was the biggest.

"Okay, boys, I fixed it. But be careful with it this time. No going over jumps or anything like that. And if it breaks again. Take it to the dump. Can't fix it anymore. I'll put this on your bill. Go have fun. And don't run anyone over. Keep it under forty."

We promised. We always promised.

This boat Mr. Burrows was building—out of iron—was huge. And even with my pea brain, I knew that iron doesn't float. I wanted to tell him, but he fixed our axle. I didn't want to hurt his feelings. I get it. I hate when someone younger than I am tries to tell me something I don't know. I think they're fibbing. Just trying to sound smart, and they're not. That's probably how he'd feel.

Now, nine out of ten young boys want to be firemen. That's what it said in a book. On Starr Hill, it was ten out of ten. We were born that way. Probably 'cause most of our fathers are volunteer firemen.

"Hey, what we gonna call us selves?" Mikey asked while picking his nose.

"We already did that dummy," I said. "It's the Starr Hill Volunteer Fire Department."

"What's volunteer mean?" Mikey asked. Still picking.

"It's like you wash the dishes before your mom asks you to."

"I don't want to wash dishes, so let's don't volunteer," Mikey said.

"Golly, just 'cause you're small doesn't mean you have to be that stupid too. Volunteer means you do good things for people before they ask you. Stop asking them dumb question. Starr Hill Volunteer Fire Department is the name." Bingo said. "Let's move before the grown-ups get home from work."

"Okay. Buddy, you've started more fires than anybody," I said. "So, you're the fire starter. You need to build it right in the middle of Park Street. Right by your house. A big one. Cardboard boxes and wood. Anything that will burn. Big. We need a real fire to go to."

Buddy left the gang to find boxes and wood. Bingo, Mikey, Bones, and I went looking for something to carry water in for our fire truck. Then we need some small cans that we could use for our fire hoses.

We found a huge—really huge—glass bottle that used to have pickles in it. Well, it still did. We dumped them out. They were probably no good anyway. Then we dug a soup can and a tuna fish can out of the garbage. The tuna fish can stunk. Those could work as our hoses.

We loaded the big glass bottle onto the fire truck and had Bones hold on to it like it was the Queen's crown. Then we filled it up with water using buckets we lugged down from our basement.

We were all set.

One street below Nelson Street—which was the highest street in Juneau was Park Street. That's where we were. The plan was to go down Nelson. Take a left down Starr Hill. Then turn left onto Park Street. We had to make that turn. If we didn't, we'd be flying straight down the hill and probably end up seeing Dr. Whitehead... which would be bad. But hey, at least the hospital wasn't far.

"Mikey, go down and tell Buddy to yell fire when he got the fire going. And tell him to yell loud. Got it? Can you remember all that?" I asked.

"Yeah, tell Buddy to yell fire as loud as he can. See? I'm smarter than I am," Mikey replied.

Bingo and I sat on the step going up to our house waiting for that call. Bones was sitting on the fire truck with that big glass jug of water between his knees. He hadn't said a word. He usually can't stop talking. Maybe he was taking this volunteering seriously.

"FIRE, FIRE!"

Bingo and I jumped off the steps. I plopped into the driver's seat of the fire truck. Bingo started pushing to get us going. After he had us up to speed, he jumped on the back and started sounding like a siren.

Blister, Buzzy, and Dumpy were playing that stupid game where you throw a rock in a square. Then you jump with one foot 'til you pick it up and jump on the other foot 'til you get back to the start. Really a dumb, stupid game. They were in the road. Playing. In the way.

Bingo had the siren going. I yelled, "Get out of the way—we're going to a fire!"

The girls jumped back, stuck their thumbs in their ears, wiggled their fingers, and stuck out their tongues at us. I knew then what it felt like to be a hero.

I turned left down Starr Hill. If we had long hair, it would've been going straight back. But all we had was stubby hair. The skin on our face looked like we were hanging our faces out of an airplane.

I had to make that corner. I knew it. I pushed hard with my right foot—it was turning, but slowly. Mead Apartments was on the corner with a white fence circling it. Our left two wheels weren't even on the ground. I heard a loud knocking sound.

"Bingo, what's that pounding sound?"

"It's Bones' knees. They're hitting the water jug," Bingo replied.

I saw it. The fire. Buddy was running toward us yelling, "FIRE! FIRE!" He was going so fast that the bottoms of his pants and his shoes were actually on fire. He ran right past us, still yelling.

"Thanks, Buddy! You don't have to yell fire anymore—we see it! We'll put it out!" I shouted. But I could still hear the thumping... and it was getting faster. And louder.

"Brakes! BRAKES!" I screamed.

We all slammed our feet down on the dirt road. Trying to stop the fire engine. We called them our sole brakes. Bones lost his right shoe, but he didn't quit. We skidded to a stop just inches from the fire.

It was a blaze now. Buddy had put too many boxes on it.

Bingo and I jumped off. Bingo grabbed the soup can, but I grabbed the tuna fish can. It stunk! We dipped the cans into the glass bottle that Bones was still holding. His fingers were white, his eyes were the size of garbage can lids, and his knees were pounding on the pickle jar.

Bingo was throwing water from his soup can and

the fire was getting bigger and hotter. I only had the tuna can, and it didn't hold enough water to put out a match. But I kept throwing water on. Then the fire spread to the side of the road. Some old moss and dry grass started burning. We were in trouble. Bones just sat on the fire truck. His knees banging on the half-empty water jug. He hadn't said a word. I don't think he had blinked since he sat down.

All of a sudden, I heard words my mom doesn't even let me *think* about saying. I looked up—and there was Art, the guy who owned the house just beyond the fire. He was cussing like crazy and swinging his jacket at the flames. It worked. He got the whole fire out and started helping us. Still cussing.

Art put his jacket back on and just stared at us. "Okay, boys, enough is enough. I'm going out on the boat tomorrow. and I don't want to worry about you starting a fire and burning our house down. Can you give me your word that you won't start anymore fires?"

"We're sorry, Art. Thank you so much for helping us get this stupid fire out. We could have done it, but we would have had to call the real fire department. Don't worry, we're going to do something else."

Art walked back to his house.

I pulled and Bingo and Mikey pushed the fire truck up the hill and onto Nelson Street. Bones still hadn't blinked. Or even noticed his shoe was missing.

"Eerie eerie!" Golly, Bingo sounded really good as a siren.

"Hey, Bingo, knock it off!"

"That's not me—it's Chief Bernie! Are we in trouble? You think Buddy's in trouble? We better stop or Chief Bernie's gonna throw us in jail," Bingo said.

We pulled over to the side of the road. Wherever the side is. It's all dirt.

Chief Bernie got out of his car and slowly walked over to us. He stood there looking at Bones. Then he moved his hand back and forth in front of Bones' face.

Bones just looked straight ahead. Didn't even blink.

"Is he okay? He's missing his right shoe. Where'd he leave that?" Chief asked.

"Yeah, he just lost it. We'll find it," I said.

Then he looked at Bingo, me, and Mikey—who was back to picking his nose.

"What do you knuckleheads have in the pickle jar?" Chief Bernie asked.

"A little water," Bingo said.

"Hmmm. And what were you doing with a little water?"

Bingo and Mikey both looked at me.

"Aw, we were just driving. Practicing with it," I said.

"Tell me, boys—what are we practicing?"

"You know. Driving and practicing. We like doing that. Practicing."

"We have a little problem here with this practicing," Chief Bernie said. "Hazel—you all know Hazel—called our office and reported some little boys were running around Starr Hill setting fires. AND their house almost caught on fire. If it hadn't been for Art, their house would've burned down, and they would've died in the fire.

Bingo was looking at Mikey. Mikey was looking at me. I was looking for a place to hide.

"Now, I don't think Art and Hazel were in any trouble. But I feel you three boys—and that stiff sitting on your cart—were playing firemen. So, we have to figure out what we're going to do about this situation. Anybody have an idea? Now's the time to speak up. Might help on the punishment."

Bones finally moved. He shook his head no. He was still holding the water jug. His knees had slowed down to a slow drum roll on the glass jar.

Finally, Little Mikey said, "Well, maybe we could go home and think about it. My daddy could tell you what we think later. Maybe tomorrow. He's a fireman, you know?"

"That's very good, Mikey, but not quite good enough. Since I'm not hearing anything from you short firemen, I'll need your word that you'll shut down the fire department. NO MORE FIRES!! No more. That's it. I can't waste my time coming up here every time Hazel calls. What I need all four of you to do—now, not tomorrow, now—is go over to Art and Hazel's house and apologize. And boys, act like you mean it. I'll find out if you don't."

"Okay, but you won't say anything to our dads, will you, Chief? Please!" I said.

"Tell you what. If you go apologize right now—and as long as I don't hear of any more fires being started on Starr Hill—I won't say a word. You have my word. But you have to obey all the traffic laws—and NO speeding. Now go have fun and don't forget about Hazel."

Chief Bernie got into his car and drove off down the hill.

We pushed the fire truck the rest of the way home. Bones was still sitting holding the jar. His knees were still softly thumping the glass like they were stuck on a timer. Mikey had run home when our backs were turned—probably got tired of picking his nose. Bingo and I headed down the steps to Art and Hazel's house.

Hazel opened the door. I saw fire in her eyes.

"What do you little rotten boys want? You know you almost burned our house down. Art and I would've died in it! You should be in jail!"

We stood there shaking. Hazel scared us more than Chief Bernie. I tried to talk but mush came out.

"We're very sorry, Mrs. Hazel," Bingo said. "We won't ever do that again. And Mikey and Bones say they're sorry too. We have to go now. Sorry!"

Art came around from the kitchen and said, "Okay, boys, I think enough has been said. You need to play something safer—war or cowboys and Indians. And maybe get your friend to let go of that glass jar before he breaks it. Oh yeah, here's a shoe I found near the fire. Might belong to one of you."

I grabbed the shoe from Art and out the door we went. When we got to the cart, Bones was still sitting there holding the jar.

"Hey Bones. Bones! The fire drill is over. Here's your shoe. You can let go of the jar and go home."

Bingo and I looked at each other.

"We gotta think how we're going to get even with Hazel," I said.

That evening after dinner, I asked Lugnut if I could talk to him in his room.

"Could you do me and the rest of the gang a favor? I know you love to run up Mt. Roberts timberline. Could you do that early tomorrow morning and get us a bunch of snow?" I asked.

"I guess I could. But first—what do you want the snow for, and second—what do *I* get out of this?"

"Better I don't tell you. It's not bad, but it *could* be. I'll wash your car for a whole month. As many times as you want. How's that?"

"Deal. I'll have your snow by ten o'clock."

Bingo and Bones showed up right on time. Little Mikey was home probably still picking his nose.

"Hey, what you got in the backpack?" Bones asked.

"Let's go over to the garbage man's house, and I'll show you."

We went through the woods and ended up behind the garbage man's steps, right across from Hazel's. I'd seen Art go down the hill with his duffel bag over his shoulder, so I knew he wasn't home.

I opened the back pack. Their eyes were bigger than baby moon hub caps.

"No! Really!"

The Starr Hill Volunteer Snowball Department was officially in service.

And Hazel?

She never opened her curtains again without a helmet.

We weren't real firefighters,
but for one whole afternoon,
we sure felt like heroes.

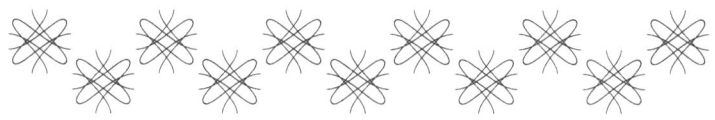

Fearless and Slightly Confused

"Hey, Blister, throw me the dumb ball! Come on, I can catch it. I'm just as good as you. The gang wants me to be their catcher," I yelled.

"Okay, okay, hold your britches," Blister said, winding up her arm like a windmill. "But you got to catch it. Won't count as a catch if you gotta run down the street and pick it up. Then throw it back."

She let it go. It was fast. I knew Blister knew that I couldn't catch it.

BAM! Right into my glove.

BONK! Right out again.

"Don't count 'cause I was watching a sea gull. You'll see—I'm gonna be the best catcher Starr Hill has ever seen. That's what Cousin Hambone said. I'll be the best."

We practiced for what I thought was hours. Maybe five minutes. Blister quit.

"I gotta go play hopscotch with Buzzy and Dumpy," she said.

"Come on, Blister, that's a stupid game. I can play with you for a few more minutes. Please. How can I be the best if you don't play with me? Nobody wants to play with me. Come on, please?"

"I promised the girls I'd come play hopscotch, so I gotta go. Play by yourself. Throw that dumb ball up in the air and try catching it. It'll be good for you."

"Hambone said I'd be the best catch on Starr Hill 'cause I got no fear. He said I'm fearless. He also said that catching the ball will come later. I'm a natural. What ya think of my catching today? Not bad, huh? Did I look natural?"

She didn't even look back. "Don't get hurt."

"Fine." I better go home and grab a jelly and peanut butter sandwich and lie down so I'll be ready for the big game tomorrow. I sure hope Hambone's right about catching will come later. I could hear the crowd as I chewed on my peanut butter and jelly sandwich.

Come on, Johnny, catch that one! Yea, Johnny! He's our hero! My head started feeling lighter as I heard those shouts in my brain. My head floated like a balloon.

Probably got too much air in there.

Next morning, I woke up when I always wake up. When Mom yelled at me. I picked out my clothes the usual way—grabbing the ones on top of the neat pile I hung on the floor. I smelled my sock to make sure they wouldn't make my feet stink. They were good. I ran down stairs where Mom was waiting with a big bowl of mush.

I hate mush, 'specially the Cream of Wheat. Mom puts all those lumps in it, and they get stuck in my throat. I want to throw up. Yuck. I'd rather have a jelly and peanut butter sandwich. It's better for you, too. I pinched my nose. Turned the bowl up to my mouth and swallowed all the mush at once.

Waited 'til I blinked twice. Then I knew it wasn't coming back up.

We were all in the Chicken Yard waiting for the game to start. The chickens were gone. The nuns had raised them and gave them to the patients at Saint Ann's Hospital. They all died. The chickens.

Basin Road Gang didn't show. Probably heard I was catching. But we had seven Starr Hill Gang members, plus Doc came up from his gang on Sixth Street. Bingo picked the sides 'cause he was the biggest. And smartest.

"Jimmie, Danny, Doc and Mikey you're on one side. Spit, Bones and me on the other. Plus, Johnny. He lowered his voice. Soon-to-be a catcher legend of Starr Hill," Bingo said. "Now we got to see who's up first. Mickey throw the bat to Bones. You two figure it out."

Mikey throws the bat to Bones. He catches the bat in the middle. They start climbing the bat with their hands. One on top of the other. The one whose hand ends up at the nob of the bat, is first. Mikey's hand is so small he squeezes it in just under the knob of the bat. It looked like they'd bat first. Then that sneaky Bones cupped his fingers over the top and yelled, "Birds' Nests." Boy, that's using the old noggin. Someone smarter than me must have told him. We're batting first.

Doc's their pitcher. He's good. Really good. I saw him pitch once. He hit the guy right in the butt when he was trying to run away.

Spit was the first batter. He swung at the ball three times, and missed. O When... the ball was on the ground. OUT!

Doesn't matter where the ball is. You only got three balls to hit. Then you're out.

Bones was next. He was so slow. Just walking to the plate made you tired. The plate was a two-by-four. Three pitches and he was out. He never took the bat off his shoulder. It didn't look good for us.

Bingo was our only hope. He stepped up to the plate. Doc threw the ball. WHOP! I heard it. But I didn't see it go. It shot out of the Chicken Yard. Landed way up on Kennedy Street. Didn't break any windows. We were jumping up and down. Wow. This was fun.

My turn. I was ready. Never batted before, but I remember what Hambone said, "Johnny is fearless," I hope he was talking about my batting too.

"Okay, Johnny, watch the ball. And swing if you think you can hit it," Bingo said.

Doc threw the ball. It went by me and Jimmie caught it. Jimmie was their catcher. I didn't even see it, and I wasn't looking at a sea gull. Strike one. I could hear Blister yelling at me.

"Hit it, hit it. Come on Johnny. Hit it."

Doc threw again. But this time I was ready for him. I opened my eyes. It went right by me. Strike two.

"Hit it, hit it. Come on, Johnny, hit it."

Doc smiled and yelled, "I'm gonna throw a slow ball." He moved his feet like dogs do after they go poop. The ball came in slow. Real slow. I think it stopped off somewhere and got a drink of water. I swung. A little later the ball went by me. Strike three.

"Next time, next time."

"It's okay," Bingo said. "Catching's your thing."

Bingo was our pitcher. He's good. He's fast. I hope he can hit my mitt. We're ready. Spit and Bones were covering all the bases. Kind of. Spit had one sock pulled up to his armpit and Bones was trying to peel a banana. Bingo was pitching and me catching. Those two square heads could keep socking and peeling 'cause they're never going see the ball anyway.

Little Mickey grabs the bat off the ground and stood over home plate. That bat was as tall as he was. He used all his strength to put it on his shoulder.

I'm down on my knees behind the plate. Just like Jimmie showed me. I'm ready. I puff my chest out. Whisper, "Hit my mitt." Maybe to myself.

Bingo winds up. He keeps winding up. I hope he can hit my mitt.

"Throw the stupid ball, Bingo. My arm's getting tired holding this stupid mitt," I yell.

He let's go. The ball is white—it's fast, it's spinning, it's getting bigger and bigger. It's not heading to my mitt. Should I move my mitt? Did he tell me he was gonna throw a curve ball? If it's a curve ball, then it'll curve into my mitt. It's not curving. It should be curving. Maybe I better wait. Oh no...It's heading right...my eyes go crossed. They're following the ball.

BOINK!

I heard someone screaming. Maybe me.

"Johnny! You alright? Somebody get somebody. He's bleeding all over home plate. We got to get him a doctor," Bingo said through his tears.

I see stars. Birds. Baseballs. Seagulls. And maybe a monkey. My head is fuzzy. Where am I? Slowly I open my eyes. I see hundreds—maybe a million—eyes staring down at me. Whose are these eyes?

"Johnny, hey Johnny!" Spit said. "Can you hear us? You okay? There's some blood on home plate but don't worry about that. Little Mikey will clean it up. You want to sit up? We could go see Doctor

Whitehead. Remember what he said last month when he put seven stitches in your head from the rock fight. He don't want to see you for a year."

I sat up slowly. "O-K-A-Y. I think I'm okay. Is my nose still on my head? It feels like it slid down to my socks?"

Doc bent down. "Don't worry, your nose is still there. It's a lot closer to your left ear. I think that's your ear. You'll be fine in a month or two."

"Oh, no. Is that all my blood. Do I have any left? I think we better go see Dr. Whitehead."

Everything was spinning around and around. I closed my eyes and lay back down. I opened my eyes. All those eyes were staring at me again. I didn't see any seagull eyes. Whose were they? Maybe they liked what they saw. Maybe they think I'm the best catcher on Starr Hill.

Just... not while I'm bleeding on home plate.

You don't need to catch—to belong.

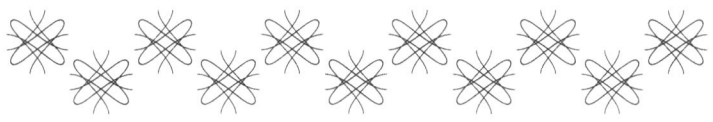

Devil's Club and Stupid Questions

Spit, Andy, Gully, Jimmie, and I were having a meeting one day in our fort. It was raining, but not pouring, so we were able to stay warm and just a little wet. Andy and Gully had joined the Starr Hill Gang.

"I think my mom is going to have a baby. I hope it's a boy," Andy said.

"Why do you think that?" Gully asked.

"Because her stomach is really big and she doesn't eat as much as I do," Andy said. "My sister said she was sure Mom was going to have a baby.

"You mean babies grow in there?" I said. "Like... in her stomach? That must hurt when she wiggles."

"Maybe you could ask Lugnut," Gully said. "He knows everything about cars, so he probably knows about babies too."

"That's a good idea. Does anyone want to smoke some Devils Club? I borrowed some matches out of my dad's back pocket so we could smoke," Jimmie said.

"Yea, let's." Andy said as he grabbed one of the dried hollow club sticks (we called it a pipe, like a peace pipe) and stuck one end into his mouth.

Jimmie took the matches out of his pocket and struck one on the lighting pad. It fired away. He held it under the pipe and Andy started puffing. He puffed and puffed. Smoke started to come out his mouth. Then his nose. His face turned an ugly shade of green.

He passed it to Gully who did the same. Gully was gulping the smoke and waving his hands in the air. First, he was red. Then purple. And finally, the ugly shade of green.

Gully passed it to me. The pipe had flames shooting out the end. I stuck it in my mouth and tried to suck some smoke in. "HOT! HOT!" I threw the pipe down, stomping and coughing. I didn't know what color I was, but I felt like it might be an ugly shade of green.

"Hey, I didn't get any, and I brought the matches," Jimmie cried.

We couldn't say anything. We coughed for ten or fifteen minutes, and then we started to laugh. Andy and Gully weren't green anymore. So, I must have become normal too.

"I got to get home and make sure my bedroom is clean before Mom gets there," I said. I'll ask Lugnut how you can tell if someone is going to have a baby. See you guys tomorrow. Thanks, Jimmie, we'll save some good smoke for you tomorrow."

It took me two minutes to run down the mountain to our house. My room was a mess and I had twenty minutes before Mom got home. I got busy. Shoved everything under the bed. She never looks there. I stood up and looked around. Spotless.

Lugnut was home before Mom. Yapping on the phone like he was getting paid for it. I needed to ask him but he just kept talking. How can anyone talk that much?

"Hi, honey, how was your day?" Mom said as she walked through the back door. "Oh, I see Wayne's on the phone, so let's go in the living room so you can tell me about your day."

We talked for a long, long time. Mom did all the talking. I agreed with everything she said.

Lugnut hung up the phone handle and started to walk upstairs to his bedroom.

"Hey, Lugnut, can I ask you a question?"

"Come on upstairs. I have to get these dirty clothes off and get ready for baseball practice."

I walked into his bedroom as he was changing clothes. "How do babies come out? You know. How do you tell if someone is going to have a baby? Or maybe they're just fat."

"Go ask Mom. She knows more about that than I do," Lugnut said.

"Yea, but you know about cars. What's the difference?"

"Babies aren't cars, dummy. Go ask Mom."

I walked downstairs. Mom was busy in the kitchen. I hated to ask her a question when she was making me something to eat. Maybe we'd have jelly and peanut butter sandwiches for dinner. That thought got me excited so I just blurted out, "How do we get babies?"

Mom stopped cutting up the lettuce. "What did you say?"

"Ah, how do you tell when someone is going to have a baby or they've eaten too much. Andy said his mother might be having a baby 'cause she doesn't eat and her stomach is sticking out of her shirt. So, what you think, Mom? Oh, and don't tell me that story that you bought me in the hospital. After two years of telling Blister I was as old as she was, Lugnut and Blister sat me down and told me it was another Santa Claus story. I want the real truth."

"Honey, I'm busy trying to get your dinner together. How ab..."

"Are we having jelly and peanut butter sandwiches for dinner? Oh, that's great. I'm hungry."

Mom turned around and started cutting the lettuce again. "Let's talk about the babies after dinner when your Dad comes home from work. Then the both of us will explain it," Mom said.

After dinner Blister got the cards out of the drawer. We played *Triopoly*. Except Lugnut. He had to go play baseball. *Triopoly* was one my favorite games.

Mom and Dad must have forgotten how babies came around, 'cause they didn't say anything about them. I was too busy trying to win the game. Blister won.

Oh, why don't I ask Blister tomorrow. She's a woman. Well, a small, tiny woman. Maybe a "gonna be" woman. I'll ask her before her bad mood sets in. It always sets in when I ask her a question or knock on her door.

Maybe it's just looking at my face.

I didn't get answers.
But I got a clean room and a sandwich.

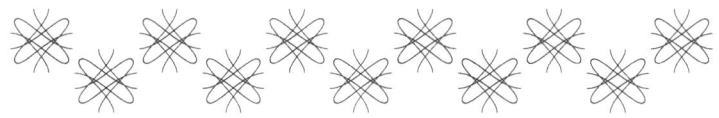

Five Floors, One Gang, Zero Adults

One of the first things you learn as a gang member, especially in the Starr Hill Gang, is how to build a fort. Not just any fort—a secret, sturdy, semi-watertight hideout where no grownups or girls are allowed unless invited. And we don't do a lot of inviting.

At first, Bones and I built what we called "fern forts." They were cozy, kind of. We'd pile big ferns and bigger skunk cabbage leaves over spruce branches, then crawl inside like happy little beavers. Problem was, the second it rained—and it rained every five minutes—the ferns turned to slime and the fort dripped green goo down our necks. We'd look like we lost a wrestling match with a septic tank. Our moms said we smelled like it too.

Still, fern forts had one big advantage. They were free and nobody got mad when you took plants. But they only lasted about four days. That's when we decided to build something better. Something drier. Somewhere that more of us could get in out of the rain. And smoke our peace pipe.

We found the perfect place for a fort. It was on the fourth switch back from the start of Mt. Roberts Trail. There were four spruce trees perfectly spaced for a fort. Lugnut and his gang had built a small one-story fort there years ago. Dad made them take it down when they quit using it. It was our turn.

We needed wood.

Problem was, wood didn't just lie around waiting to be taken and turned into a fort. It usually belongs to some old grouch.

"We could use the leftover wood from that new house that's being built near the Evergreen Bowl," I said. "You know that guy who works at the Empire Paper. He's always yelling at us when we try to borrow some of his crummy crab apples. Let's take his wood instead of those apples."

We borrowed our Dads' hammers, without them knowing, and marched off like a little army of mini-carpenters. When we got there, it was like finding gold. The lumber was all stacked up and ready to be taken. Untouched. We didn't need the hammers after all.

We were about to start loading the lumber when a big man, with even a bigger voice, came out from behind the house.

"You boys must be looking for some lumber to build a fort. Am I right?" he bellowed.

"No sir. I mean yes sir. We were just drooling over your, uh...pile," I said.

If he'd been ten minutes later, we would have had brand new boards to build our fort. Oh, well. Least we didn't get caught borrowing them.

"I'm going to start taking the old boards off this house in the afternoon. You're welcome to come by tomorrow and take as many as you want. Watch for the old nails. I'm not going to pull them out for you. And don't even think about borrowing a couple of new boards. I have counted them so I know how many are there. Besides I know all your dads, so let's plan on seeing each other tomorrow."

That last part hit like a hammer to the knee cap. "Thank you, sir," we all said in unison. "We wouldn't dream of taking any new boards. Could we have the old nails? Our dads are running a little short of them."

"Take as many of the old nails as you want. You know how to straighten them out so you can use them again, right?"

"No, could you show us?" I asked.

He took an old nail that had a big bend in it and put it on a piece of wood with the bend sticking up in the air. He grabbed his hammer and held one end of the nail and hit it on top the bend. Wow! It flattened out. That looked easy. I bet even Mikey could do that.

The next morning right after we played a game of basketball in the Chicken Yard, the four of us headed toward our wood supply. Mikey was the smallest one so we put him in front. We loaded up some long two-by-fours and a few slats of shiplap onto the shoulders of Mikey and Jimmie and sent them on their way. Bones and I grabbed some short boards of shiplap and headed to the fort. We got there the same time Mikey and Jimmie did. We were ready to start building.

We started building the first floor using "Starr Hill Engineering." We weren't gonna be like those stupid architects from America. They made flat roofs. They didn't know it rained in Juneau every day. Now if our fort leaned only a little, that was good. As long as it didn't fall over.

Andy and Spit joined us once we finished the second floor, which was also the roof for the first floor.

"What's this?" Andy asked, trying to stand up.

"That's the second floor," Bones said. "It's a little short. You gotta walk like you're a crab."

After another week, we had four floors. Each floor was getting smaller. And wobblier. We couldn't stand up in the second or third. In fact, we could only stand up in the first floor. Not really stand up. We could only stand up on our knees. But Mikey could stand up on his legs. He was short.

Good thing we got all those old bent nails from Ralph the wood man. Our dads were not happy with us taking all their nails, plus losing a few hammers.

I told my dad about the missing hammer, but I'd find it when we cleaned up around the fort.

"Find them now!" he bellowed.

"I will Dad. They're probably right by the saw and square."

"SAW!"

"Dad, it's okay. We didn't use the square. And I'll find all of them."

I found them. But was told I wouldn't be using any of his tools again.

No one. Not the Basin Road Gang, not the Gastineau Avenue Gang, not even the Gull City Gang had built a four-story fort. We'd be the first in the Territory of Alaska. And we'd be higher than the Mendenhall Apartments. It had twelve floors, but it wasn't as high in the air as ours. It helped that our fort was built on the side of Mt. Roberts.

"Yeah," Bones said, "but we got a better view. If you climb to the top, I bet you could see Canada.

And maybe into the Evergreen Bowl."

Just when we thought we were done, Spit thinks we should go one more floor. So, we built a fifth floor just big enough for Mikey to crawl in. On his tummy.

We pushed him up. "Hey, Mickey, you like it up there," Bones yelled.

We heard him mumbling. Guess there wasn't enough room for Mikey to move his jaw. So he stayed. Listening. Breathing.

"Hey, we should celebrate," Andy said. "Let's get some Devils Clubs and have a smoke out. Come on. I got matches."

We all gathered on the first floor. I know what a sardine feels like. Bones lit the match and Andy started puffing. All of a sudden there was a moaning sound. Maybe a thumping noise too. Somewhere.

"Oh, no. We forgot Mikey. He's stuck upstairs," Spit said. "We smoked him out."

Andy squeezed up to the fourth floor and grabbed Mikey by the shoe. It stayed. But Mikey came crashing down. A red and green face. Coughing. Crying.

"Mikey, you want to smoke some Devils Club?" I asked.

Mikey went running down the trail crying. Missing one shoe. I took that as a no.

We did it. We built the first Skyscraper of Starr Hill.

It leaned a little. Okay. A lot. It smelled like wet socks and smoked Indian rhubarb. It creaked like Mom's knees and groaned like Lugnut when he had to do dishes.

But it stood. Five glorious floors of splinters, stolen wood, and bent nails. It wasn't pretty. It wasn't safe. But it was ours.

Then Dad found it. He looked up at it for a long time. Then he looked at me.

"Is it...supposed to do that?" he asked.

"Do what?"

Right then, the top three floors shifted and fell down to make it the second roof. It didn't look good.

One whole summer we had spent building this. It only took seconds to come down.

The fort leaned.
So did we.

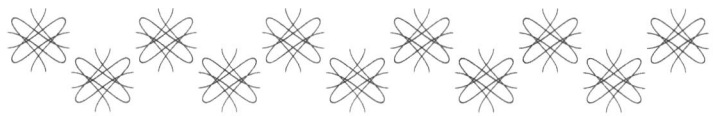

How We Got Our News

Our meetings at the fort had three solid purposes. Maybe four if you count yelling at each other. First, to smoke some old Devils Club and pretend we like it. It was disgusting. But we felt important. Second, we swapped stories or gossip that our Moms and Dads had talked about the night before or before the night before. Third, we tried to outsmart each other with big grown-up words we didn't understand.

That's how we got our brains to grow. By listening to our parents. And how we got as smart as some of the grown-ups. The ones that weren't brain dead.

My brain was getting bigger every day. I was sure of it. I remember when I was younger, my dad was always calling me "pea brain" 'cause my brain was still small and mostly filled with cookie dust. Sometimes in the morning I'd check out the mirror. Couldn't tell if my head was getting any bigger. Hard to say for sure, but I felt smarter. Sometimes there was rattling or sloshing in there. I knew something was working. And my dad didn't call me a pea brain any more. He now used bigger words. Some I couldn't pronounce. Or spell.

That morning, rain was bouncing off the ground. We were supposed to meet at nine on the first floor of the wood fort. Our fort had five floors thanks to five Starr Hill Engineers. I put my boots on and Lugnut's old rain coat and headed up to the fort. I slipped with every step I took. I was worried nobody would show up not because of the rain, but the wind was blowing so hard the garbage cans were rolling down the street.

I wasn't sure what time it was, but I knew it wasn't time for lunch. My belly always told me when it was noon time. Finally, I heard Bones yelling my name. He must have been lost. He'd been here hundreds of times, but maybe his brain wasn't growing as fast as mine.

He walked into the fort on his knees. "Hey, why we meeting? It's raining like the dogs and cats, mostly dogs," Bones said. "I could have stayed in bed."

"Boy, that's exciting. Hey, Andy and Danny are coming. Danny said Freddy is going to sneak out and meet us here. Freddy's dad works for the city so he always has funny stories to tell. Soon as everyone gets here, we'll smoke the peace pipe and find out what our Moms and Dads know. Then you can go home if you want."

A couple of minutes later, Andy showed up.

"Holy cow! It's raining bears and porcupines," Andy said, as he brushed aside the blanket we used for a door. "My dad said it rained so hard last night that a house near Gold Creek washed away. It's out in the ocean now. Hey, John, can you see it from your house?"

"I can't even see the water. The clouds are zooming by like they're late for dinner and there's not gonna be any planes landing in the channel because of the rain and wind."

"Once, I didn't see it happen, but I know it happened. A Grumman Goose landed and flipped over 'cause he landed with his wheels down. Guess he thought he was landing at the airport and not on the water. What a dummy."

Then Freddy ducked through the blanket door. "Hey guys, I had to wait 'til my dad left. Dad was yakking all night. Laughing so hard I thought he'd fall off the kitchen chair. Had a story about the city workers."

"What he say? What he say?" Bones asked.

"Hey, don't tell the story yet. Let me get my knees under me," Danny said as he folded his knees and shoved them under his butt.

Fred looked over at Danny and started talking. "Dad said the mayor was so tired of hearing about the city workers not working that he had some signs made."

"What the sign say?" Bones asked.

"If you let me finish, I'll tell you. Dad said the Mayor had twelve signs made that said Men Working. The city workers were supposed to put them out next to wherever the guys were standing around holding shovels so folks would think they're working even if they weren't."

"I don't get it. That's the dumbest idea I've ever heard of," I said. "You pretend to work by putting up a sign that says you're working. Like wearing a shirt that says I'm doing my homework while picking your nose."

"We should go and see. But not today. Pass me the pipe," Danny said as he pulled his knees out from under him.

"Anybody hear anything else?" I asked.

"I want to go home," Bones said. "I'm cold and my underwear is soaked."

"Yea, this is stupid," Andy sighed. "I'll see you tomorrow if it quits raining. Then we can go watch the city men put those signs out. Then maybe we'll know something."

Grumbling and soaking wet, Bones and Andy crawled out of the fort. Danny followed, dragging his knees like they been run over by a street grader.

"See you guys tomorrow," Freddy said, "unless I drown trying to cross the Chicken Yard."

"Yup," I said. "Tomorrow, we watch city workers not work. Should be educational."

I looked around at our soggy, smoke-filled fort. I was the last one left. Sitting cross-legged in a puddle. Smelling like wet Devil's Club and burnt skunk cabbage.

If this was how grown-ups learned to get smart, no wonder they drank.

Wet feet, warm hearts, big ears.

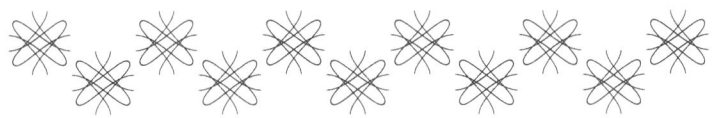

Word of the Day

There was a little rain coming down when we got to our meeting place. We just built our new fort the day before, so it should last for a couple more days. It wasn't too slimy. This one was made out of limbs from a big green tree and ferns that had blown down in a storm last week.

"I heard my dad talking about the Chief of Police," Jimmie said. "He said the Chief was going to quit if he didn't get his way."

I broke in. "Yea, my dad talked about it too. Said that Bernie told somebody that if they made prostitution against the law, then a terrible disease would take over the town, and the politicians would be the first to get it. It might be mumps. I don't know what disease he' talking about."

"What's propotition?" Mikey asked.

"I think it means when those ladies who have a red light above their door wave at you. Dad and I drove by once, and they we're all waving and smiling. Dad used that big word but said they were very nice ladies.

"Oh." Mikey replied. "I don't know about that disease, do you?"

"I do. It's when you get a bad bug and your pee-pee falls off. I heard it's really bad. I don't want it," Bones said.

Bingo nodded like a doctor. "I heard it was called "Gonaweewee."

"Let's find out what the disease is so we don't get it. Maybe it's in the fort, but we don't know it," I said.

We all jumped up and looked at the ground where we'd been sitting. It was a short meeting.

Two days later, the gang decided to have another meeting. This time up Mt. Roberts at the first picnic ground. There were five of us there: Spit, Bones, Buddy, Bingo and my best friend Doc. Oh, yea, and me. Now six.

Jimmie had a cold. Guess we needed to give him a dirt pie so he could make the next meeting. Mikey was playing inside because it was raining, and he wouldn't go outside if his brother didn't. If we stayed inside every time it rained, we'd never play outside.

"I got an idea. It's a good one too," Spit said. "My mom said we should pick a word we don't know and all of us look it up in the dictionary. Then talk about it at our meetings. We would get really smart that way, and we'd be way ahead of the other kids when school started. Maybe even smarter than our sisters."

"That's a great idea," Buddy said. "But what if we don't know what the word is."

"Let's use a word that our mom and dad talk about at dinner. Last night my mom said Dad was constipated. Does anyone know what that means?" Bingo said.

"I think I don't know what that means," Buddy said. "That makes it a good one. Maybe we can use it."

"Does anyone know how to spell it and where do we find out what it means?" Doc asked.

"In the dictionary stupid," Bingo smarted off. "Ours is red. There are blue ones and black ones. They don't have as much meaning in them, so get a red one."

"Okay, but we better not meet 'til next week 'cause it's going to take a while to go through all those words to find constipation," Spit said.

When I got home, I asked Mom if we had a dictionary. "I need a red one."

She went to the book case and got out a big book and placed it on the table. I smiled. It was red. I was already smarter.

"What word are you looking for in the dictionary?" she asked.

I told her the word we decided at the fort was constipation. Maybe she could tell me so I wouldn't have to look it up.

She giggled, really giggled. Like a little girl. "Do you know how to spell it?"

"Nope."

"Do you know what the first letter is?"

"C" I think. "Mom, I need you to help me."

"Lucky guess," she said. She flipped through the pages, no pictures, just lot of black squiggly words. I hate books without pictures.

"Okay, I will write it down and then you can look it up in the dictionary. Have you ever looked up a word in the dictionary?" she asked.

"No, but I looked up cowboys in the other big books."

"I think we'll do this together. I'm proud of you for wanting to learn new words. I wish you would have chosen a smaller word, but that's just me."

Constipation, here it is, she said. "Difficulty, incomplete, or infrequent evacuation of the bowels."

"Is that English? Does it have a meaning? Can we use it? Huh, Mom?"

"Couldn't you boys find a different word? A word that you can understand?"

"No, Mom. We need to use words that you and Dad and other parents are using so we can be smart too. Please help me. Still don't know what it means."

"It means, oh for goodness sake, it means, for your fort meeting, it means you're uptight. Okay. That's all you need to know."

We met again at the first picnic grounds on Mt. Roberts. Everyone made it, including Jimmie and Mike. It wasn't raining.

"I found the word in the dictionary. You guys want to know what it means?" Bingo asked.

"I didn't know I was supposed to bring a word to the meeting. Someone should have told to me," Jimmie said.

"Well, if you're playing sick how we suppose to tell you. Just listen and maybe you'll be smarter after we tell you the word," Doc said.

"Yeah" echoed around the fort.

"Go on, Bingo, what you saying."

"Well, it's a little more complicated than you think. So, I won't quote the dictionary. I'll explain it so you can all understand it. Constipation means that you can't go number two."

"Did you have a red dictionary?" I asked.

"Don't matter the color of the book, it's what's inside it."

Man, I bet Bingo is gonna be a lawyer or something some day when he's older. He's already two years older than I am. Glad I didn't say anything or tell them what Mom said.

"Okay," Spit said. "Let's find one that we can use all the time not just when my dad can't go number two."

"Anybody got a stupid idea?" Bones asked.

We all raised our hands

The dictionary was red.
Our faces were too.

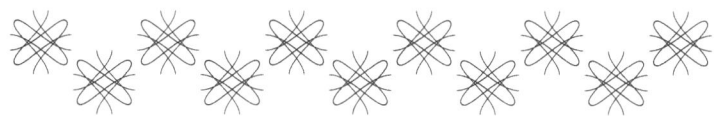

The Blue Bike and the Man Bar

"Hey Dad, when do I get a bike like Blister's. Sorry, I mean Carla. She's had one for years, and I have nothing. I've been good. So how about it? Huh, Dad?"

"I'll talk with your mother, and we'll see if we can come up with something for you," Dad replied.

"Thanks, Dad. You missed my birthday, but any day will work. Just make it blue. I don't want a sissy bike like Carla's. You know where they don't have that man bar in the middle. It's gotta be a big boy's bike. But blue. Okay, Dad. Please. I'll finish my dinner every night."

"You know your Mother has the final say in everything. But I'll talk to her. So, you better be on your best behavior. What's this "man bar" thing? I've never heard of that. Is this another one of the things you made up?"

"No, no Dad. Lugnut said girls' bikes don't have that metal bar in the middle of the bike. They call it a man bar. Girls don't have it so they can wear a dress and pedal. And I don't wear dresses."

"Sometimes you surprise me with your smarts."

"Gotta go meet the gang. Tell Mom only blue. You won't forget will ya, Dad?"

"Go play."

A week went by. Nothing. No bike. No blue. No man bar. No nothing. Maybe Dad forgot or maybe he was in the dog house also.

I was moping around the house when Lugnut came storming through the door. "Hey, kid. You see what's outside in the yard?"

"I know. Mike left a pile on the stairs' Mom told me to clean it up, but I didn't get a bike. Not even a blue one. So, I don't care. Nobody cares about me. That's probably why Mike pooped on the stairs. He knows I'm mad."

"Quit being a baby. Babies cry. You won't get a bike if you cry. Now go look."

I shuffled towards the back door. My head was drooping down so far it looked like I was sweeping the floor with my hair. Oh poop, I got to go clean it up. No bike. My life was over.

I headed down the stairs. My eyes were fixed on a pile that Mike had left on the stairs.

Then something sparkled. I glanced over.

A bike.

Blue. A blue bike. With a man bar. And wheels.

"Lugnut, Lugnut, it happened. It's right there in the yard. Is it mine? Oh, thank you! It's blue."

"Don't thank me. You better thank Mom and Dad. They're the ones that bought it. It's a used bike, but it's still in good shape. Let me change into some different clothes, and I'll come out and put the training wheels on for you."

I was standing by the bike. Just staring at the blue. Petting it like I did Mike. Where was he going to put the training wheels? It already had two wheels. There wasn't room for two more.

Lugnut came down the stairs, taking two at a time. I wish I could do that, but my legs were too short. He went into the basement. A few minutes later he came back out with a huge wrench and two little wheels with metal arms. Those were too small to do any good.

He flipped the bike upside down in the middle of the street. No cars ever came up here. It was a short street.

He got to work putting two little wheels on each side of the back wheel. I was getting worried. I couldn't ride it like this. Even if he put the wheels under the seat.

Lugnut was smart most of the time, but I was worried now. Then he picked the bike up and turned it over. Wow. My brother's a lot smarter than older people. The back wheels now had little wheels to help it go.

"Hey kid, you ever ride a bike before?"

"No, but I see Blister riding all the time. If she can do it, I know I can do it. I'm better at things than stupid girls." I grabbed the handle bar and sat on the seat. My feet barely touched the pedals.

Lugnut had a hold of the seat of the bike and my shoulder.

"Okay, I can go. Let go. Lugnut, let go."

"I'm not holding you back. You have to pedal to make the bike go. Push forward on the bike pedal and keep doing that and you'll go. To stop, push on the back of the pedal. That'll stop the bike. Whatever you do, don't—and I mean don't—go down Starr Hill. You'll be back seeing Doc Whitehead. Or we'll be burying you alongside your blue bike. Got it?"

"Yea."

I started out slow. Real slow. This wasn't easy.

Push down on the pedal, check.

Don't drive into anything, so far check.

Push back on the pedal to stop, panic.

My hands were doing one thing, the front wheel was doing another. My brain was spinning like a merry-go-round. Too many moving parts for my little brain to control.

I finally made it to the end of the street. Felt like I'd biked to Canada. Too many things to remember. Got off the bike. Turned it around. Street was narrow. All afternoon, back and forth, forth and back.

The next morning, I strutted into the kitchen. "Hey, Lugnut, can you take those baby wheels off now? I think I'm ready to be a man."

After he got those wheels off, I began to worry. Maybe I should be a little boy one more day. There were no wheels to break my fall. No. I was big now.

I put my right leg over the man bar 'cause I was right-handed. Then I pushed off with my left foot and down on the pedal with my right. I did it. I was riding with no baby wheels. Slowly. I only fell over once. Maybe three times. I lost count.

The next day, I was feeling brave. I looked to see if anyone was watching me. I was good. I felt like I was leading a parade. Then my brain, the one that decides things in a second, decided to go faster. I stood up on the pedals. Started peddling as fast as I could. All smiles. I let go of the handle bar with my left hand and waved. For only a second.

Suddenly, my right foot slipped off the pedal. My leg went down toward the ground. I landed on the man's bar with the middle of my body.

WHAM!

I hit the dirt bank, tipped over, and grabbed where the pain hit hardest—right between my legs.

Couldn't breathe. Couldn't scream. Couldn't do anything but leak tears from my eyeballs and try not to cry 'cause Lugnut said, "Little brothers don't cry."

I stood up. Sort of. Climbed back on and started peddling again. Every bump felt like someone was driving nails into me. Oh, it hurt. But I knew, deep down, this is how to get better. One painful pedal at a time.

After riding all afternoon, I walked home. Bow legged. Just like those cowboys I've seen in the movies. Just in time for dinner. I wasn't hungry. I couldn't sit on a hard chair. I wanted an iceberg.

"Are you ok, honey?" Mom asked, trying not to laugh.

"Yea, just a little sore, but I'm fine. I think I will go to my room and not eat anything. I might have a stomach ache."

"Okay. But you can come down later. I made some peanut butter cookies. That might help."

I "cowboy walked" up the stairs to my room and gently crawled up onto the bed. I was afraid to take my pants off. I was afraid of what might or might not be there. I lay on the bed for a long time. Sweat was running off my forehead.

I couldn't stand it. I had to peek. I unzipped my jeans and hung them up on the floor. No blood. Whew! I felt better. I slowly lowered my underpants.

Oh! My goodness. Black. Blue. Everywhere. My legs were the same color as a pigeon's neck. Oh no. I couldn't show Mom. I couldn't show anyone. They'd put me in the hospital, and I'd never ride a bike again.

I climbed back on the bed and fell asleep. I guess the pain was sleepy too.

The next morning, I ran into Dad on the way out.

"Hey, Dad, I gotta cut it off. It hurts too much"

His face went white. Like he'd seen a ghost or a grizzly bear. "YOU WHAT? Don't you cut anything off. You need that for the rest of your life."

"Do you understand?" Dad said. He seemed upset. I didn't know why. Just cutting it off shouldn't hurt.

"Dad, I don't want to hurt myself anymore. I want to cut off the man bar and then I can ride better and not hurt anymore."

Dad froze. Then he cracked up. He laughed so hard he had to hold onto a chair. Tears ran down his eyes.

"What so funny?

He wiped his eyes. "You, son. You."

And that's what love is:
A blue bike, a bruised butt, and
a Dad who laughs 'til he cries because
you scared the life out of him just trying to grow up.

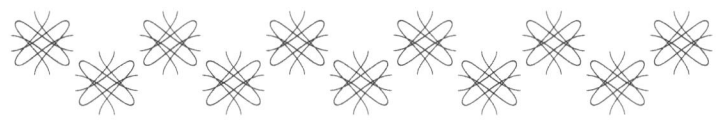

Angel Hair and the Devils Itch

Today finally arrived.

"You up, John?" Dad yelled.

"Yea."

I'd been awake for hours. Maybe all night. I climbed out of bed, grabbed my long-johns that I piled neatly in the middle of the floor, and pulled on my jeans. Opened the bottom drawer and found two pairs of socks. Didn't want my feet to get cold. My shirt hung over the chair, but I put on my t-shirt first, then my logger shirt that had the red and orange squares. I was ready. I threw back the curtains, hoping Joyce, who lived next door, might be looking out her window so she could see what a real logger looked like. She was old like Blister but a lot cuter.

"Wayne, we have to eat first, then we'll head out. Yell up to your little brother. Better yet, go up and make sure he's ready to go," Dad said.

Just as I headed down the stairs, Lugnut was coming up.

"Hey, we got to eat. Then we can go," Lugnut said.

"Can I sit in the front seat with Dad?"

"Not this time. I'm driving and Dad always wants to be in the front seat in case I do something stupid," Lugnut said.

I had my logger breakfast. Two eggs, yellow looking up at the sky, on two pieces of white toast covered in ketchup. When you stirred up the yellow and ketchup, it looked like someone poured blood over a dandelion. As soon as I put my plate in the sink for Mom to wash, we headed out the door. Lugnut stopped in the basement and grabbed a hug hand saw and met us at the station wagon.

My heart couldn't stop making my shirt jump. I knew I was getting older. This was an honor I'd waited for my whole life.

"Wayne, remember we're not in a hurry, so keep an eye on the other cars. For God's sake don't knock off the side mirrors on the bridge."

I was standing up in the back seat. I didn't get to go over the Douglas bridge very often. And I couldn't figure out why they called it the Douglas Bridge. When you were in Juneau headed to Douglas, they called it the Douglas Bridge. But when you came back the other way, they called it the Juneau Bridge. When my brain got larger, I'd figure that one out.

We made it across the bridge, both mirrors still on. We took the road to the right that headed out to North Douglas. We drove a long time when we came to a small meadow along the side of the road.

The snow had stopped falling, but the ground had over two feet of snow. Lugnut parked the station wagon just off the road. Good thing Lugnut put the chains on. We all got out. Lugnut grabbed the saw. Off we went into the wild.

We walked for hours. Trees everywhere. Some were as tall as I was. Most taller. My legs were getting tired.

The snow was almost in my front pocket. I looked over at Dad. He had short legs too, so I knew he was tired.

"Wayne," Dad puffed, "we need to find a tree. Let's not walk around the whole island looking for one. It's just a damn Christmas tree."

"Hey, there's one. It's a beautiful Jack Pine!" Lugnut blurted out.

I looked up. And up. Where we going to put this tree? It was bigger than our house and the station wagon didn't have enough room for the tree and me. I wasn't staying out here.

"Good God, Wayne, that's way too big," Dad said.

"Dad, look at it. It's beautiful. We're not taking the whole tree. I'll cut halfway down from the top," Lugnut said. He started cutting before Dad could say a word.

"TIMBER!" I yelled as the tree fell over. That's what a real logger sounded like. I always wanted to do that. Lugnut trimmed some of the branches and grabbed it by the bottom limb and started walking back towards the car. Dad and I just carried ourselves. That was enough.

By the time we got to the station wagon, Dad had smoked four Camels. Must have been giving him a lot of energy, but he was still huffing and puffing... the whole way home.

Clank. Clank. Clank. I put my hands over my ears.

"Dad, I better pull over and wire that chain link up. It'll be okay 'til we get home. Then I'll take the chains off and fix them," Lugnut said.

We paused by the St. Ann's Hospital before going up the Starr Hill. The snow was coming down hard now. No car tracks going up. Lugnut took a deep breath. I squirmed in my seat. This was gonna be great if we made it. I held my breath.

Lugnut took off. We're doing two hundred miles an hour when we hit the bottom of Starr Hill. Up the hill we shot. Fish tailed all the way up. I put my gloves back over my ears. All the chain links must have broken. Lugnut would need to fix both sets.

I exhaled. "We did it, Lugnut. We didn't go back down that hill backwards. Good going. You're a good driver, isn't he, Dad?" I said.

Dad mumbled something. I don't know what.

"Grab the saw, kid," Lugnut said, heading up the stairs with the tree.

I followed him and dropped the saw by the basement door and shadowed Dad. I had to get my shoe packs off. I knew I'd find icicles for toes. Mom fixed some hot chocolate, and then Dad and I huddled around the oil stove. I was colder now than I was when we were outside.

We left the tree in the basement for three days. On the third day, Lugnut stood the tree up in the middle of the basement. Looked for places where he needed to put limbs. He cut off part of the bottom. Suddenly we had lots of extra limbs.

"Let's put one here, Dad," Lugnut said as he turned the tree. "Here's another spot." He found five more places he wanted to put branches.

"Okay, okay! Looks fine to me. If you want to put in all those extra limbs, you're on your own," Dad said. "The drill and bits are in the blue box under the work bench. I'll take the tree stand upstairs and get the living room ready."

I stood around mostly. Taking up space and asking stupid questions. I knew they had to be stupid 'cause no one ever answered me. Besides, Lugnut was busy cutting limbs, drilling holes, then trying to fit the limbs into the tree.

"I think we got it," Lugnut said. "Go up and open the doors and make sure Mom doesn't have anything in the way. Especially on the table. She's still mad about that plate I broke last year."

I ran up and opened the porch and the back door. I cruised through the kitchen. There was a plate of cookies on the table. I grabbed two and shoved the other five in my pocket. If anyone asked, I'd say they fell on the floor. I put the plate in the sink.

Lugnut came through the door dragging the tree. Dad had put the tree stand down in the middle of the living room. Right where Mom wanted the tree.

"John, lie down beside the tree stand. When Wayne lifts it over the stand, guide the bottom of the tree into the stand. And watch your fingers. Don't let them get in the way," Dad said.

"Ouch! Oh! ME FINGER! Darn me finger in the hole! Lift the tree! Hurry! Hurry! Now!" I screamed.

Lugnut lifted the tree and set it on the floor by the table. "You okay?" Lugnut asked.

"What'd I tell you, John. You have to use your ears for more than a pillow. Please, try listening once in a while rather than talking all the time. You see any blood?" Dad asked.

I was afraid to look at my fingers. I knew they were gone. Finally, I opened my hand and there were five fingers.

"I think I need a band aid. A big one."

"Let me see," Dad said, and grabbed my hand. "You don't need a band aid. Tell Mom to wash the blood off your finger. A pine needle could cover that scratch."

I ran into the bathroom where Mom washed my cut with peroxide. It foamed up into little bubbles. Then she put on a band-aid. A really big one. I knew Mom was smarter than Dad when it came to band-aids.

By the time I got back, the tree was in the stand and looked beautiful.

"We gonna decorate it now?" I asked

"No, we'll wait 'til your sister gets home. We all need to do the decorating," Mom said.

Blister didn't get home 'til dinner time. She was always late. So, Mom decided we'd decorate the tree tomorrow. I didn't want to talk to Blister. Darn her. She always ruined everything for me.

The next morning, I could smell the Jack Pine all through the upstairs. I headed downstairs. Looked out the front window. Blizzard. I couldn't see the telephone pole in front of our house. I wanted to sled.

"Where you going?" Blister asked.

"I'm going sledding. The gang will be coming out of their houses, and I want to be the first one down the hill."

"You don't want to decorate the tree? Good. I'd rather do it with Mom, Dad, and Wayne anyway. Go play."

"Nah, I don't have to be first. But if you would have been home on time, we could have decorated the tree last night. I'd be sledding right now."

"Oh, poor you. Go get the lights out of the box."

Lugnut came down stairs and started stringing the lights out in a line on the floor. He plugged one end into the wall. Nothing.

"See what you did, Blister, I said. "The lights don't work 'cause you were late coming home last night."

"John, help your sister," Lugnut said. "It's not her fault. These lights are old and just burn out. Get the extra lights out of the box and pass them to me when I ask for them."

Good thing Lugnut was here. The lights might work.

We got all the lights working. Dad and Lugnut put them up on the tree.

"Now what?" I asked

"Calm down. You're worse than a fart in a hot skillet," Dad said. "We're going to put up the ornaments. First, we'll put up the snowflakes your mother made. Then if there's room, you and Carla can put up some red and blue ornaments. Can you handle that?"

"I got to go help Willie," Lugnut said as he was walking out the door. "Leave the Angel Hair for me 'til I get home."

"You and me, Blister. I better be the boss 'cause you don't know how to put things on a tree. I'm a logger."

"You're nothing but a big pain in the butt," Blister said.

We placed Mom's snowflakes on the tree. That wasn't easy. We had to bend a piece of wire then push it through the snowflake, then hang it on a limb. Blister decided we needed to put only blue balls up. The first one I picked out of the box jumped out of my hand and crashed to the floor.

"What was that? Mom asked. "You have to be careful handling those ornaments. Some of those belonged to my mother years ago. Please be more careful."

"Wasn't my fault Mom. Blis-Carla asked me a question. Before I could answer, the ball just rolled out and fell on the floor. I can be better. But tell Carla not to talk so much."

We hung five balls. All blue. Then came the icicles.

Blister told me to sprinkle them. I grabbed the box, ripped off the top, and pulled out the icicles.

I threw them in the air toward the tree. Those that didn't make the trip, I'd pick up off the floor and throw them higher up the tree.

I was about ready to go sledding when Dad came in the room.

"What have you two done. Have you ever seen icicles go sideways? This looks more like a spaghetti tree than a Christmas tree. Don't let your Mother see this. Pull those icicles down and put them back on the tree. One at a time. Just like Wayne told you. Carla you know better."

"Sorry, Dad. This is the only time in my life I followed John's advice. I promise it won't happen again."

I looked out the window. Blizzard. Four of the gang were sliding down the hill. Spit had his new sled, the Silver Streak. I needed to help him in case he let me ride it. I headed for the back door.

"I gotta to go, Blister. If there's any icicles left, I'll fix them when I come back. Thanks, Blister."

After dinner, I waited 'til nine o'clock for Lugnut. I wanted to help with angel's hair. I'd never seen it before.

Finally, my eyes couldn't stay up any longer. I started to walk up the stairs to my bedroom. The back door opened and in walked Lugnut.

"Hey, I've been waiting all night for you. I want to help you put up the angels with hair."

"I don't know if that's a good idea. What did Dad say?"

"Oh, yea," he said, "whatever Wayne says is good with him. So, if you say good, then Dad's good, and I'm happy and good. Let's put up the angels. We already got one on top of the tree. What are we going to do with the other one with hair?"

"It's not an angel. It's called angel hair. Why don't you watch me this year, then next year you'll know how to do it? Sound Good?"

"Yea. Maybe. Okay. I'll watch but if you need help, I'll be right beside you. Blister has gone to bed. Did you know she was late the other night, and that's why we didn't decorate the tree? Stupid. Girls!"

Lugnut opened the bag and pulled apart the hair real slowly and draped it over the lights. It looked like colored fishing line. But smaller around. He turned on the lights. When they came on, they were all different colors and shined every which way. How did he do that?

Lugnut, did that to all the lights. All but one. I didn't tell him he missed one. I'd tell him in the morning.

"Lugnut that's the most beautiful tree I've ever seen. I bet Santa, I know there's no Santa, but if he came to our house, he'd take that tree with him to show off to the whole wide world. And he'd say we did it together."

"Thanks, kid. I'm going to bed. Shut off the lights when you are done. Oh, don't forget to unplug the Christmas tree lights. See ya in the morning."

Soon as he left, I went over and pulled the bag of angel hair out of the box. I took out a handful and stretched it out just like he did. I placed it over the light he missed. I stood back and drooled at my work. I didn't want to go to bed. The tree smelled so good, and now I could say I decorated it with angel's hair.

About two in the morning, I woke up itching—arms, belly, toes. Even inside my ears. I couldn't stop. What did I have. I was about to wake Mom when I remembered what Lugnut said. "Don't get this on you or you'll itch yourself to death. It's real glass that they shaved to make thin so light will pass through it."

As I scratched between my toes, I thought, why do they call this *Angel Hair*, it should be called the *Devil's Hair*!

Next year, they can keep their Angel Hair.
I'll just draw a halo with a crayon.

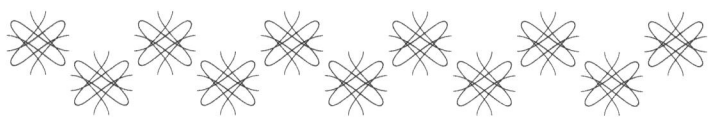

Not All DA's Are Cool

My brother Lugnut has the coolest hairdo. A DA. That stands for a Duck's Ass. Mom doesn't like us to say "ass" in our house but DA is okay. She don't know what it means.

All the cool older guys like Lugnut have 'em. They comb their hair slicked back on the sides so it meets in the middle, then use their finger to draw a line right down the back like a little duck's butt strutting across their skull. I'd only seen the rear end of a duck after Lugnut shot one, and, trust me, dead duck butt wasn't quite as glamorous.

Lugnut even had the walk to match. He said it was a swagger, but it looked more like a stumble from a Dad who'd had one too many. Not cool.

I want to be just like them. And the real cool ones would put a package of Lucky Strikes in their rolled-up t-shirt sleeve. Now they looked like James Dean. Especially if they're smoking. I hadn't smoked yet, but I was already planning on being a Lucky Strikes Man. LSMFT: Lucky Strikes Means Fine Tobacco. I heard the guys at the gas station laughing and saying, LSMFT really means, Loose Straps Makes Flabby Tits. Better not tell my mom that.

Dad smokes Camels. I haven't had either one. Yet.

Having a DA meant everything to me. I might be only eight and a half but I knew I needed a DA. Only problem, every time my hair got long, Mom would grab the clippers and zip, gone.

I needed a plan to stay out of her way, so I could let my hair grow out. I started hiding. Behind couches, under beds, in closets. Anywhere I could grow my hair in peace. Finally, after months of dodging scissors, I had enough hair. It was now long enough to be called slick.

One afternoon, I caught Lugnut staggering through the living room heading towards the bathroom to look at himself in the mirror.

"Hey, Lugnut, how do you keep your hair curved around your head? And shiny? I need mine to look just like yours," I said.

"You really wanna know?" he said. "Gotta to promise you won't tell Mom. Okay? I mean it. If you squeal, I won't ever take you up the mountain with me. You promise?"

"Yes, I promise!" I blurted out. My heart was beating faster than a chipmunk's. I'd be the first one in my class to have a DA.

"First," Lugnut said, "you need grease that works with water. Next, wet your hair. Comb it back around your head. Now this is the important part. Take that grease and pat your hair with it. When you're done patting your hair, run your comb through it again. Might take a couple of times to train your hair. Be sure to wipe your comb on your pants. And don't get that grease on Mom's towels," Lugnut said. "You got that? DON'T GET GREASE ON MOM'S TOWELS!!"

I nodded like I understood every word he said. I didn't. What's the name of grease? Do I say anything to my hair when I'm training it? I knew one question might be one too many for Lugnut. But just finding out how to do the DA was the most important one. I could figure out the other parts.

I spent the next week looking for where Lugnut hid the hair grease. He's always hiding things from me. Once, I found my white hanky in his back pocket. I didn't use it. I threw it in the laundry.

After searching Lugnut's room when he wasn't home and digging through the medicine box and finding nothing, I headed to the basement. That's where Lugnut spent all his time when he was home. Working on something that had to do with cars or boats. After going through all of Dad's shelves and drawers and crawling under the work bench, I began sneezing like a baby elephant.

Then I saw it.

A blue and white can. "Water Pump Grease." Those words said it all. It was made by Standard Oil of California. Probably in California. That's got to be it. The word water on the label. Yes! Jumping up and down. I knew I had my grease. What else would cool cats use? I had found heaven.

The next couple of days were spent in front of the mirror training my hair. I'd wet it. Comb it back. Pat it with my hand. Then say "stay." It didn't. My hair flopped forward like it was trying to escape.

Then I remembered Lugnut said to pat the grease on. That was the part I forgot. Comb it back. Train it. The talking to it was all my idea.

I was in the basement playing basketball with a tennis ball and a pickle jar. Mom's words floated through the floor boards. Excitement came over me like a snow blizzard.

"Honey, it's time for bed. Wash up and don't forget to brush your teeth," Mom said.

Grabbing a handful of grease, I ran upstairs. Snuck into the bathroom and began wetting my hair patting the grease in. Then I used Mom's comb and ran it through a couple of times.

"Stay" I whispered.

And it did.

My DA was perfect. So was I.

I wiped the comb on my jeans and carefully put it back on the dresser. I grabbed a bar of Ivory soap to wash off the grease off my hand. But the grease wouldn't leave. Instead the grease climbed onto my other hand. I grabbed my toothbrush and brushed my teeth. I tried to put it away. Nope.

That's when I realized it didn't want to leave my fingers. Without thinking, I grabbed the towel and took the toothbrush off my fingers. Oh no.

Now I had a greasy towel. I rolled it into a ball, put in under my arm, and headed to my bedroom. Then threw the towel under my bed.

I tried taking my clothes off. But my fingers were stuck to the buttons like bubble gum. Forget it. I went to bed fully clothed.

I couldn't go to sleep. My little brain was doing backflips, like squirrels eating peanut butter. Mom always said to count sheep. I tried once but only got to twelve or thirteen and then I run out of numbers. Or sheep. Finally, I was out.

Until my eyes flew open.

Something was wrong. My eyes rolled around in my head looking for a dead animal. I tried sitting up, but my head leaned to one side.

I became frightened. My hand flew up to my right ear.

A pillow was stuck to it. I yanked it off. My hair came with it. Placing the pillow back on the bed, I noticed it was brown and sticky. And stunk like a dead squirrel. Or maybe a fish.

Now I had a pillowcase and a towel to hide from Mom. I hid them both under the bed. So far, my plans were not working. If I could sneak out and get to school, things would be cool.

No sound came from the kitchen. I tiptoed down the stairs. Put on my boots and slipped out the back door.

There was a man and woman walking down the road just in front of me. I knew they were Russian 'cause my dad said that Russian wives always walk two steps behind their husbands. So, they were Russian.

"Morning, Mr. and Mrs. Scott," I said.

They looked at me...then elbowed each other and started to snicker.

Everyone on Starr Hill came from Russia. Or somewhere like it. Chek-o-slo-voka. Or U-go-slo-vahia. Hard words to say. But I knew what I meant. Anyway, I'm sure they thought I was cool.

I got to school and all my friends were in the backyard playing "Red Rover." I ran over to join them.

Turning towards me, they began pointing their fingers at me and laughing. I bent over to make sure my fly was shut. It was. The laughter was getting louder and louder.

I ran into the school bathroom. I could still hear them laughing. Looking in the mirror, my mouth fell to the floor.

Oh, no! My hair wasn't blond anymore. Yukky-yukky crusty brown. Greasy spikes stuck out the sides like porcupine quills.

No, no, they weren't supposed to be there. This can't be! All that training. All that talking wasted. I didn't have a comb. I never carry a comb. Lugnut didn't tell me to carry a comb. He said my hair would always stay where it was supposed to stay. On my head. Cool.

There was no one in the bathroom. Panicking I grabbed some toilet paper, patted my hair. "Stay, please stay. Oh, please let me be cool." It stayed... along with the toilet paper.

I needed to escape. I ran out the door and didn't stop. I ran faster than my dog Mike. I could hear the laughter chasing me all the way home.

Mom took one look at me and shook her head. She seemed to be doing that more and more when I was around. Turning on the kitchen faucet, she told me to take off my shirt. When I got up on the kitchen chair, she stuck my head under the water and began scrubbing my head until I thought all my hair was leaving me for good. It brought back memories when I put creosote in my hair by accident. Luckily this time it was just a duck's ass.

"Go jump in the bath," she said. "And let's not do everything your bother does. Okay?"

"Okay, Mom."

I got a day off school. That was cool.

But I need to ask Lugnut quietly what kind of grease he used to train his hair. But I'll wait 'til Mom forgets about me.

Some lessons you learn the hard way.
Some you learn with a pillow stuck to your head!

Paratroopers of Starr Hill

I ran up the stairs into the kitchen.

"Hey Mom, Mom, could you make me a couple of peanut butter and jelly sandwiches. We're going to war. It's C day. I gotta get right back outside!"

Mom raised her eyebrow. "Did we forget something?"

I looked down at the floor. Mud. "I'll go take my boots off, but I'm in a hurry. Sorry."

She crossed her arms. "We forget anything else?"

"Oh yea, I'll go wash my hands, but don't forget I'm in a hurry."

"I'm not making any sandwiches 'til I hear those special words."

"Please Mom. Please hurry, Mom!"

Mom put the peanut butter and jelly on the counter and opened the bread drawer. Took out four slices of white bread.

"John, it's going to take a few minutes. This bread is stale I'll have to put them in the oven. It'll just take a minute."

Mom went to the fridge, took out some brown and green lettuce, and stuffed it between the bread pieces. She wrapped the bread and lettuce in silver metal paper and popped it in our oil cook stove. Mom said the lettuce would freshen up the bread. I hope she takes it out before I put it in my mouth 'cause lettuce has never been in my peanut butter and jelly sandwich before.

It seemed like hours went by. I'm afraid the war would be over before that stupid bread was done. I can't stand waiting. I kept walking back and forth through the kitchen. That smell of bread and lettuce in the oven made me hungrier.

Finally, it was done. Mom made me two sandwiches. Shoving them into my mouth and gulping them down with a glass of milk, I am now ready for war. As I headed towards the back door, Mom came walking into the kitchen. No smile.

"Forget anything?"

"No, Mom. Got my hat and my boots. I'm ready to go to war. See ya."

"Not going anywhere until I hear those words."

"Thanks, Mom. Got to go. I'm late for the war. We're jumping into Germany today!"

We've been talking about this for a week. It was Spit's idea. Right above our house stood an old house with no doors or windows. But lots of dog poop all over the floors. It stunk worse than walking through Dog Shit Alley that was next to the Red Dog Saloon. But we played in the house anyway. When it rained.

Last Saturday we saw a matinee with these American soldiers being pushed out of an airplane. They landed in a bunch of grass. They called them paratroopers. It was a special day. D-Day. Those paratroopers charged a hill shot a bunch of

"Nadsees," then stole their machine gun.

The battlefield was in front of the old house. Two gang members would get rocks and hide in the old house. That was gonna be their pretend "Nadsee" fort. Three of us would charge up the hill. Just like those paratroopers in the movie did. Shoot the enemy, and capture the fort.

"I'll be a "Nadsee" in the house. That hill is too steep for me," Bones said. "I'd have a heart attack."

"Yea, I'll help Bones and be the enemy too," Jimmie said.

"Then get some rocks for hand grenades. Not big ones. And don't hit any of us, especially you Bones," Spit said.

"I'll try not to hit anybody," Bones said.

We hurried down the hill from the old house. Bones and Jimmie loaded up on rocks. Spit, Gully, and I went looking for stick machine guns. Not just any stick. They had to be the right size, with a little branch for a trigger. We broke off all the little sticks that would poke us in the belly. That'd hurt. We found branches that made beautiful machine guns.

"You guys ready?" I yelled.

"Yea."

We got our guns and met on the wooden sidewalk that was down in front of the "Nadsee" fort. The hill was steep going up to the fort, but not too steep for us paratroopers. Bubbles were building in my stomach from the excitement.

I found a place where we could jump from the sidewalk down to the ground. I felt like I was standing in the door of a real airplane looking at those red and green lights. The green one told us to jump.

"Okay, remember to hook up to the cable or your parachute won't open."

"Where's the cable?" Spit yelled.

"Just pretend the railing is the cable. That makes where I'm standing the door you're going to jump out. Let's go."

Spit went first. I gave him a shove. He threw his gun off to the side and yelled "Geronimo!" He landed on his feet and rolled to the side picking up his gun and charging the hill.

Gully jumped next.

Then I went. "Take the hill!" I shouted.

We ran through the devil clubs and Indian rhubarb blasting our stick guns.

Bang! Bang! Bang!

The "Nadsees" threw grenades down on us. Boom-boom. Rocks were flying everywhere. It was a real battlefield.

Boom! Boom! Boom!

Bang! Bang! Bang! Boom!

"Oh no!" Gully yells out. "Your dog Mike went the bathroom over here. What do I do?"

"Go around it dummy. And be quiet," I yelled. "We're supposed to be sneaking up on the enemy. Keep firing."

Spit hollered from the bushes. "I'm in nettles. Help!"

"Bones, stop throwing them grenades. Spit ran into nettles. We need a medicine man."

"Who's the medicine man?" Spit whined.

"Gully, you're the medicine man. Rub some dirt on Spit. Make sure it's clean dirt. And hurry! We got to get up that hill."

Gully found some clean dirt and rubbed it on Spit's arms and face. He had a brown face with little red bumps poking out. Spit's tough. He jumped up and started firing his machine gun and yelling, "Take the gun—get the dummies."

Halfway up the hill, grenades were landing closer to us. I felt like a real paratrooper. I wish I had a uniform on. I'd be a sergeant. My heart was going faster than our dryer.

BAM!

I was flat on my back looking up at Spit. A warm feeling swam down my face. I put my hand to my head. Blood. Red. Mine!

"I think one of those grenades found your head. You okay? You better go see your Mom and tell her I didn't do it," Spit said.

Spit put a big green leaf on my head and was holding it with his hand as we headed towards our house. Gully was walking in front of us.

Where'd the "Nadsees" go?" I mumbled.

"Last time I saw Bones and Jimmie, they were running down the hill just like those "Nadsees." Chickens."

"I can't see you, Spit. There's blood in my eyes." I didn't hurt that much. Now I know how a bird feels when it flies into a window.

Mom opened the door. Took one look at me. Sighed, "Not again. Let's go see Doctor Whitehead. Thanks, boys. He'll be okay."

Good thing St. Ann's Hospital was at the bottom of Starr Hill. Probably why my parents bought our house.

A lady in black opened the hospital door. They called her Sister. Not my sister but someone's sister. That's kind of neat. Didn't have to remember their name. Lugnut, called them penguins. Mom said that wasn't nice and for me not to repeat it.

They put me in a little room with a window that looked out onto Sixth Street. I saw Spit and Gully.

I knocked on the window. When they turned their heads my way, I saluted. They saluted back. These were real paratroopers.

Dr. Whitehead burst into the room, "You again. You should move in. You spend more time here than at home. Let's see what you've got."

Brushing my hair to one side, he took a bottle of something hot and poured it over my head. Wow, I grabbed the chair so I wouldn't fly away.

"That might burn a little, but I have to clean out that wound. How did you get this nasty gash? Oh, don't tell me. You got hit with a rock." He never lowered his voice.

How did he know. Could he see us from the hospital?

"I'm gonna put in a couple of stitches in that square head of yours, and you should be fine. Don't go swimming, but you can take a bath. Keep those stitches dry. See you in a week. Promise me you won't be back before that."

I nodded my head slowly. Then Mom and I headed out the door.

When we got outside, all the paratroopers were waiting for me—Spit, Gully, Bones and Jimmie.

"Looks like your fellow soldiers are really some good friends," Mom said smiling. "Why don't you ask them over for milk and cookies?"

"Hey guys, you want to have some milk and peanut butter cookies. You know the ones that my Mother always puts a black bottom on."

My mom made a little groan. Huh? "Oh, yeah. Thanks for coming to the hospital, and I don't care who threw the grenade. It's war."

Mom, holding hands with me and Spit, headed back up Starr Hill. I felt tired and someone was playing drums in my head. Nothing a good paratrooper couldn't handle. Maybe I'll get one of those Purple Hearts or another peanut butter and jelly sandwich. I'd rather have the sandwich.

My head had stitches, my friends had bruises, but we all had a lasting friendship.

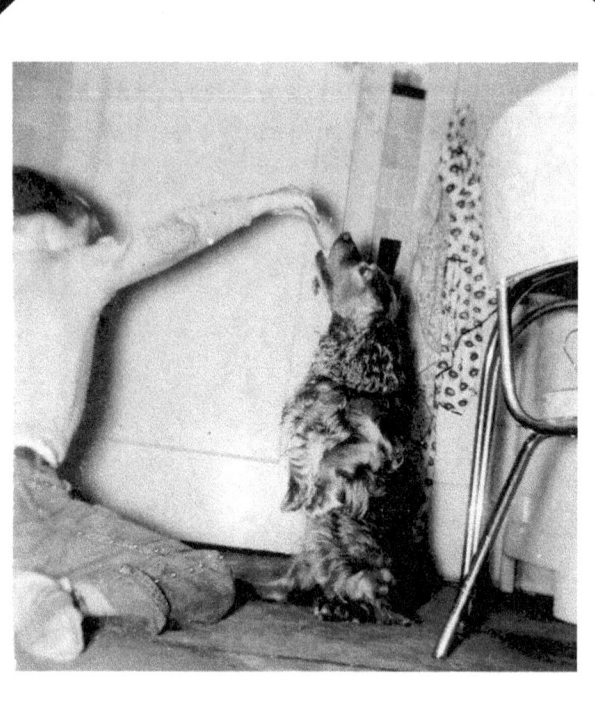

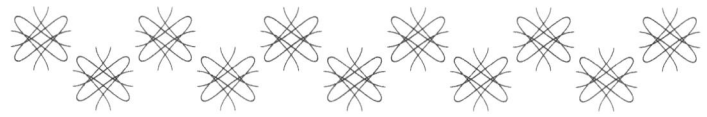

Cool Cats Give the Finger

"Hey, Lugnut, when you going to give me a ride in your old jalopy?" I asked.

"If you call it an old jalopy one more time, you'll be walking the rest of your life and that might be cut short too," Lugnut shot back.

When I grow up, I want a car just like Lugnut's. His was a shiny green 1951 Chevy with little metal flakes that made it sparkle. A white top. That way the seagull poop didn't show. No dents. Whitewalls. I really like those fat whitewalls. Lugnut had to wash them all the time just to keep 'em white, especially after every dog treated them like a fire hydrant.

I wasn't too sure about the skirts though. Not the kind girls wear—these skirts went over the back wheels. Two problems. One, they covered up the whitewalls. And two, they were called skirts. Skirts don't belong on a boy's car. If they were called "wheel-pants" or "tire shields," I'd put them on. But no way I'm letting anyone say, "Hey, Johnny...nice skirt!"

But Pipes? Oh, yeah, pipes. I need pipes. Lugnut called them Glass Packs. I don't know, maybe they're made out of glass. Who cares. But man, when he'd put the car in first gear and we cruised down Seward Street, those pipes would let out a low rumbling sound that echoed off the buildings and chased us all the way to Front Street. People turned their heads like we were Elvis and Buddy Holly rolled into one.

I'd sit there, proud as punch, dreaming of the day I'd have that sound. And maybe a girl sitting beside me smiling at me like I was James Dean. With a shiny DA.

First, though, I had to learn to drive. I'd been watching Dad. He was slow but steady like "smoke-and-steer kind of guy." He sat behind the wheel. A Camel hanging from his mouth. Following the hood ornament, whichever way it pointed.

Now Lugnut had a cool style. He always wore a white t-shirt with the sleeves rolled up. He'd slouch over the wheel. One shoulder curled around it like he was turning the car with his elbow. Had a knob on the steering wheel called a "suicide knob." Made it easier for turning. But if it caught your coat, good luck. I decided I didn't need one of those. I needed both hands to stay cool.

From his rear-view mirror hung two black and white fuzzy dice. Now that was stupid. No dice in my car.

Sometimes, not very often, Lugnut would take me for a ride "out the road." That was the only road out of Juneau. It went twenty-eight miles to a dead-end sign. You'd think if the road stopped, you wouldn't need a sign that said "DEAD END." It was on those rides that I started noticing something really cool.

Lugnut had a lot of friends.

Every time we passed one, he'd wave. But not like most people. No full arm salute or arm pump. He'd just lift one finger. Not just any finger. It was the one next to his thumb. Just a tiny, slow lift off the steering wheel. Like he was too cool to try harder.

The other guy would lift his finger. Neither smiled or made any facial expression. It was like two ship passing in the night. But instead, it was two cool dudes floating through life on rumbling engines and one raised finger.

That was something I had to learn. How to give the finger because being cool wasn't just about driving and pipes. It was about style. About mystery. About that slow finger wave. If you weren't cool, you were nothing.

Dad didn't give the finger. He just nodded like he was about to fall asleep. The other old guy would nod back. Probably too tired to lift a finger, or maybe they hadn't invented "the finger" yet when they were kids. I wonder if cowboys gave the finger when they passed each other on horseback. Probably just tipped their hat. Or grunted.

I especially liked it when a girl Lugnut knew came driving towards us. She'd recognize his car and start waving like she was cleaning snow off the inside of her windshield. Her head bobbing up and down, and smiling with big grin. Full on windshield wiper mode. I watched Lugnut carefully. He did his usual. Slowly, lifted that finger, cool as ever. She'd watch our car until it passed. Lucky there wasn't a telephone pole in her way.

When we passed, he'd push in the clutch, rev the engine, and downshift. Those pipes would growl. I'd drool.

I bet that girl would give anything to be in my seat. But I wouldn't let her.

I'd just sit there, hand on my lap, and secretly raise one finger. Not for anyone to see. Just practice.

One day, I'd give the finger. And I'd be cool too.

I didn't have a license, a car, or a girlfriend, but I had the finger. That was a start!

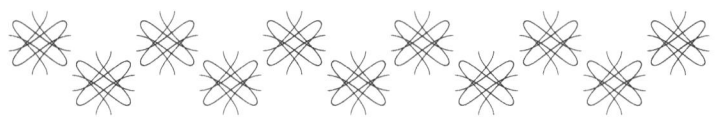

All in the Word

In May I'd be a whopping eleven years old. Two more years, and I'd be a teenager. I could hardly wait.

I was walking home from school when my brother Lugnut pulled up in his '53 Chevy and leaned out the window.

"Want to ride out the road with me?"

I'd ride anywhere he went. "Thanks, Lugnut."

I ran to the passenger side. But there was already someone in my seat. A girl.

She got out and pulled the back of her seat forward. Motioned me to climb in. I started to, then my eyes clamped on to another girl sitting in the back seat. I climbed in and tried not to act surprised.

Lugnut said the girl in front was Malin. Her sister, who was now sitting beside me, was Sue.

I'd never sat that close to a girl except in school, but she didn't make my head itch. My eyes kept crossing trying to look at her while not turning my head. She was cute. More than cute.

After we dropped the girls off at their house, we drove back to town.

Lugnut said, "Hey, you should ask Sue out. She's a looker."

Girls. Ugh!

My brain remembered what it said in the car—she was more than cute. And she made my stomach curdle. Not like getting sick...more like...happy gas pains. You know, a nice but weird feeling. But she was a whole year older than I was. One year. That might be a problem. I doubt if she would even look at me, let alone go to a movie or be seen in public with a younger boy.

I told Lugnut about the age difference. "One year don't mean anything," he said. Of course, he left out the part where his older girlfriend dumped him after a month.

The next day I got to school ten minutes before she did. Sue lived out the road so she had to take the school bus. I waited for her to get off the bus. I wanted to make sure this is what I wanted in life. When she stepped off, I decided yep! This was happening.

As I walked home from school, I decided I'd call her. I practiced talking out loud what I was going to say. "Hi Sue, my name is John Bertholl. I'm a year younger than you, but I'd like to go to the show with you."

That's stupid. That didn't sound like me. She knows I'm a year younger. "Sue, how would you like to go out with me or, better yet, meet me at the 20th Century Theater."

Now that's more like me. Show you're not just a boy but a short man. The closer I got to home, the braver I got. I had everything under control.

I ran around the house making sure the house was empty. I didn't want anyone to hear me. I took the handle for the phone off the wall. I was shaking. I put it to my ear.

"Operator. What number please?"

Her phone number was black. Ours was Blue.

Black and Blue. That had to mean something. Like salt and pepper. Maybe peanut butter and jelly. Yes, elbows and scabs.

Sue's number was Black 1222. Mine was Blue 400. And that B? That B meant destiny.

I felt like we were practically engaged. I mean... our numbers started with the same letter! That had to count for something. Was it fate? Or love? Maybe it was...long distance, but still.

I could feel my heart thumping so hard it made my shirt pocket puff out. No one answered. My shirt pocket quit moving. Then I remembered she had to take the school bus home. I waited another half hour. I couldn't wait too long because my mom would be home from work. I couldn't let her know I was talking to a girl.

A half hour crept by about as fast as a glacier melts.

"Hello."

A log jam began to build in my throat. I tried swallowing. "S-S-Sue." I garbled out.

"Yes?"

"Hi, this is John Bertholl. My brother Lugnut, I mean Wayne Bertholl, said I should call you and see if you wanted to look at me. I mean talk to me. Can you do something like that?"

She laughed. "Yes, my sister Malin said you might call." She seemed so calm. Nothing like the blubbering idiot that she was talking to.

"Then... you like me?"

More laughing. "You're funny. Listen I have to practice my saxophone for an hour before Mom gets home from work. Maybe we could talk at lunch tomorrow?"

"Yeeess. Okay, then lunch. Bye!" I did it. I did it. She likes me. Oh god help me. Please make me good.

I was now on my second job at eleven years old. Folding popcorn boxes at the Twentieth Century Theater. Juneau had two theaters. Capital Theater on North Franklin Street and the Twentieth Century on Front Street. I liked the Twentieth better. Both theaters had cats to keep the rats out. That caused a small problem for me—I was allergic to cats. But I needed the job.

Danny, my friend from Starr Hill, and I had to fold two hundred popcorn boxes every Saturday for the next week's shows. And for that back-breaking job, we got free tickets to the movies, along with a coke and popcorn. Sometimes.

Sue and I talked at lunch and agreed to meet before the matinee outside of Percy's Café, which was next door. She and her friend showed up. I gave them both a ticket. In public.

Excitement, along with fear, filled my head. I didn't know how or what I was supposed to do or say. I should've watched a western and see how the cowboys did it, but one wasn't on 'til after our first date.

I then ran back into the theater. I stood behind the curtains and waited until she and her friend Beth sat down. Slowly the lights lowered. A huge roar of a lion echoed in the theater. The curtains went back into the walls. A picture of a lion's head appeared on screen. Then, throughout the theater, little heads began scurrying around. Just like when we shined the car lights on at the garbage dump. The rats were running all over the place. I joined the other little heads, found a vacant seat next to Sue, and sat down.

Danny was two years older than I was and was already sitting next to Beth.

"Hi Sue," I squeaked out.

"Hi, John. Didn't know if you were going to sit with me or not," Sue said.

"Agh, yea. Do want any popcorn? Maybe a Coke?"

"That would be nice. And just a small Coke," Sue replied.

I ran up the aisle to the concession stand. Sweat was rolling off my head. I stood by the popcorn machine. Day dreaming. Wow. Finally, I collected all my marbles and got in line. My friend wasn't working, so I might have to pay for it. When I got to the front of the line, I ordered a small popcorn and a Coke.

"That'll be thirty-five cents," the girl said.

Oh, I only had twenty-five cents. "I fold popcorn boxes, so I get a free Coke with my popcorn."

"Who told you that?"

"Ray, he's the owner."

"We're busy. So, I'll let it go this time, but I'm going to talk with Ray.

I grabbed the Coke and popcorn and made a beeline for my seat. I passed the popcorn to Sue and eking out a smile I said, "Any time."

I sat there breathing very heavy. Today was going to be the day. I had talked myself to sleep every night with this plan. Bravery had to overtake fear.

Then came the Newsreel. Tanks. Men in hats. Somewhere in the world things were blowing up, but all I could think about was the plan.

This was it. I told myself all week during "Old Yeller" that I'd touch elbows with her.

"You want some popcorn?" Sue asked.

But I panicked. She passed me the popcorn, and I grabbed for her hand instead. It wasn't the plan. It just happened.

She didn't move it.

I couldn't move.

She didn't pull away.

I stared straight ahead. I couldn't speak. I didn't breathe. But I was holding a girl's hand. In a theater. During a movie. At eleven years old.

We were one.

That Hand?
Still Holding It Today!

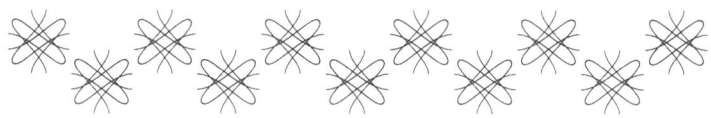

Poop, Feathers and Romance

Lugnut was out working in a logging camp, so I had the use of his bedroom. Not to sleep in, just to sneak in and mess with.

Before he left, Lugnut had been feeding pigeons, much to my dad's disgust. Don't blame Dad. Pigeon poop looked like oatmeal flung at the window by a crazy person. He wasn't wrong. But that gave me an idea.

It was Monday, Mom was at work and Blister was still trying to find her way home from school. I had a plan.

I met Sue at the Saturday matinee the previous Saturday. During the Newsreel, they showed how important pigeons were in the Second World War. They trained them to fly messages back and forth to the front lines. While stuffing popcorn in my face, a thought popped into my brain. What if I trained one of those pigeons to deliver letters to Sue? Telling her how cool she was. She lived five miles "out the road." Imagine her opening her front door and there on the front porch was a pigeon with a letter dangling from his claws.

"Dear Sue, you are more beautiful than a salmon berry in full bloom." I was excited.

I wanted to run out of the theater before the show even started. But it was *The Deep Six*. I never missed a good war movie, especially with Alan Ladd in it. *Shane, Come Back, Shane.*

On Monday, as soon as school was out, I made a beeline for home. Lugnut's bedroom window was a slider. Got a board from the basement about two feet long by a foot wide. Placed it just inside the window frame for a perfect pigeon runway. I sprinkled some popcorn on the window sill, then onto the board leading inside to his bedroom. Standing behind the curtain. I waited.

Ten minutes went by. Nothing. I was about to give up when this beautiful pigeon landed on the window sill and began eating. She had shiny, purple-green feathers on her neck and a head that bobbed like she was listening to music that only she could hear.

I imagined she was saying. "Train me, train me."

Slowly, with her head bobbing, she peeked around the window. Her eyes widened. All clear. She slowly bobbed her way in. She cleared the window slide. I slammed the window shut. My pigeon, who I thought wanted to be trained, ignored my wishes.

She took off like Jet Blue. Flapping down the hallway towards the tiny window at the end. She slammed into it like a bowling ball. She fell to the floor, then tumbled down the stairs into the kitchen. I was right on her tail. Feathers flying everywhere.

She got back up and soared through the kitchen, leaving feathers and poop behind. Into the living room. BAM! Smack into the bay window.

This one hurt. She hit it so hard that more poop and blood flew out and landed in Dad's favorite chair. Enough feathers to fill a pillow were now in the air. She needed a blood transfusion. I had to get her before she pooped again.

One more time. It wasn't far to a window behind the couch where she got herself tangled up in the curtains. Her flight lessons were over. I slid the couch forward, reached down, and lifted her up. Gently. She was nearly featherless.

She looked at me with those cold brown eyes. Her head lay at a funny angle but had quit bobbing. I took her outside. Sat down on the steps with her. She rested in my lap.

"Go. Go fly. Do something. Get out of here. My Mom's coming home, and you can't be here. I'm so sorry. I only wanted you to take a letter out to Sue's."

I picked her up again and took her down to the landing by the basement and set her in some soft grass and moss. Could she fly with five feathers? I hope so. But I knew I had to give her back to nature.

Four o'clock. Oh no! Mom would be home in forty-five minutes. I grabbed the ammonia from under the sink and proceeded to clean the blood and poop from the windows and floor. Then on to Dad's chair using the same rag.

I was now old enough to run the bigger machinery in the house, so I got out the vacuum and operated it like it was a front-end loader. Every time I thought something was clean a feather floated by.

I glanced out the window. Mom. Two blocks away. I was moving faster than a squirrel. I looked out the side window. No pigeon. I breathed a sigh of relief. Hopefully, she found somewhere warm to recover.

I listened as Mom climbed the stairs. The door opened. A feather slowly floated towards the ground. I grabbed it in midair and stuffed it in my back pocket, along with the other hundred or so feathers.

"Wow," Mom said. "What have you done?"

My heart stopped. Another feather floated by when she shut the door.

"What did you spill?" Mom asked. "And where in the world did you find the ammonia? I've been looking all over for it."

"Oh, ah, you said if I had some time I should try helping you out. Just thought I'd do a little cleaning."

"That's nice, honey. Thank you. When I was walking up the stairs, I saw old Fred's cat out in the yard. He must have gotten himself another bird. He had a feather dangling from his lower lip." Reminded me of Bert and his Camel cigarette. I almost started to laugh.

"Mom, I got to run down to the basement, be right back."

I got to where I had put the pigeon. He was gone. Hearing a noise, I looked up, there on a telephone pole sat a pigeon. Was that her? Or was she in the tummy of Fred's cat?

I decided...

I had love in my heart and poop on the curtains.

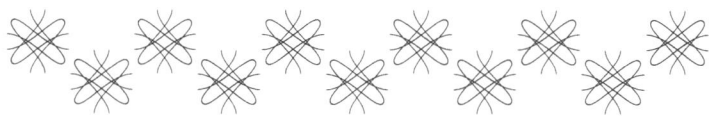

The Big Move

In 1957 there was talk around Juneau that Alaska was going to become the forty-ninth State. I didn't care. Becoming a state was not going to help me with my problem today. Sue and I were sitting in the 20th Century Theater waiting for the movie, T*welve Angry Men* to start. I didn't care if there were twelve, fifteen, or one hundred angry men. All I cared about was whether I was brave enough to hold hands the right way today.

Today had to be the day. For the last few months, Sue and I had been holding hands. The regular Methodist style. Palm together, fingers flat. Respectable. Boring. Like you did with your mother when she took you downtown as a little boy.

But today had to be different. I needed a going steady style. That's when you interlock your fingers, so the feeling from each finger flows through to the other one's finger and then rushes up to that soft spot in your brain. With love. That's what Spit told me. He should know, 'cause he's always reading those mushy books.

"If your fingers ain't tangled, you ain't trying," Spit said.

If the cartoon had been Road Runner, I would've made my move when the coyote fell off a cliff. But no, it was Tom and Jerry. Ugh!

Still I could feel Sue was waiting for me to make the move. Her fingers were relaxing, like they were whispering, "Come on...grab me, hold me, make me go steady." I reached into her popcorn bag. Our hands touched.

Sue looked at me, smiled, and I imagined her dreaming *she'd be going steady before the show got over. I know she thinks I'm cool.* I'm not. I'm a fried egg sizzling in a hot fry pan. Without ketchup. This was the longest day of my life and probably hers too. I've never wanted something so much.

Tom and Jerry was over. I felt done. The curtain closed. Then the roar of lion came back and the curtains slowly opened. The movie, *Twelve Angry Men* starring Henry Fonda flashed across the screen. Starring Henry Fonda. Who cares. I needed just a few moments of quiet to put my plan together. Sue looked at me thinking, "What are you scared of little boy?" She's running out of patience. I feel it. I have to move. It's now or never. What if it's never. That would be the end. Move! Now!

I wiggled in my seat and reached into her popcorn bag. Again. We smiled at each other. Again. I chewed slowly, I didn't want this moment to stop.

Her fingers relaxed a little more. I'm thinking she wants my fingers. She needs my fingers to go steady. My heart is pounding so hard my shirt has a bump in it. And moving. Will my heart leave before we go steady?

Move your fingers, stupid!

I wiggled again. Just a tiny bit. I let go of her left hand to scratch my right ear. Seems like my hand has been scratching for a long time. Sue looks at me with those eyes that say, "I'm ready big boy."

    I lowered my hand. I found her left hand right where I left it. On the arm rest. I can feel her smile. I know it's big. It's time. I slowly put my fingers in between hers. I drew my first breath in what felt like an hour. Or more.

    Our eyes locked on each other. Smile. I know she's thinking. "He's all mine. I never have to worry about the other girls. Steady we go.

    I'm already thinking what my next move will be. Putting my arm around her. My biceps start to slowly rise. I lift my elbow two inches and…that's as far as it got.

Our fingers said yes,
before our mouths did.

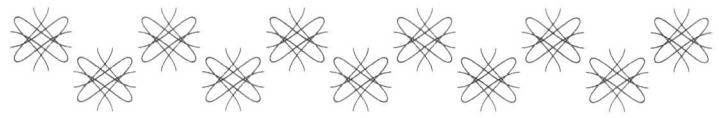

Fishing with Lugnut

The first fishing trip Lugnut took me on was out to Salmon Creek. Salmon Creek was about three miles out the road where the creek runs on both sides under the bridge. We had to hitchhike. That was another first. I'd never hitchhiked before. I was excited. We walked down to Glacier Avenue and right across from where they parked all the big trucks to plow snow in the winter. This is where we started hitchhiking.

"I want you to stand behind me and do everything I do. Can you do that?" Lugnut asked.

"Yea."

"Okay. We'll face the cars when they are heading out the road. Stick out our right thumb and move your hand just a little. Smile. Keep walking backwards or the drivers of those cars will think you are lazy and won't pick us up. Whatever you do once we get a ride, don't start yakking like you always do. Okay?"

"Yea."

The first car came, and we put out our thumbs and walked backwards. He must have not liked the looks of Lugnut 'cause he didn't even slow down. We kept walking. More cars went by. Then an old red truck pulled over. "Where you boys headed?"

"Salmon Creek," Lugnut replied.

"Hop in the back."

After Lugnut set both fishing poles in the back of the truck, we jumped in. So far, I didn't have to carry anything.

I didn't say a word. There was no one to talk to except Lugnut, and I knew he'd tell me to hush up.

I'd never ridden in the back of a real truck before. I'd ridden in the back of Dad's Model A but that was a lot smaller. So was I. Didn't know where we were going. Just that it was called Salmon Creek.

This was fun. My hair was blowing in the wind.

The truck dropped us off just before Salmon Creek Bridge. We jumped down from the truck, and Lugnut thanked him for the ride. He waved. Off he drove. We walked down to the edge of the creek. There were other boys fishing, so I wasn't worried about getting lost. Lugnut took two halves of a fishing pole and stuck them together. He pulled out some line off the reel and put them through the eyes on the pole. Then he tied a hook to the line, put a small piece of round lead on the line, and put some eggs on the hook. Not regular eggs but little itty-bitty tiny ones. Soft. He showed me how to cast the line out into the water and how to turn the reel handle forward so the hook came back in—without the eggs. From then on, I had to put on my own little eggs.

Lugnut fixed a pole for him and threw his line out in to the creek for about ten minutes. He didn't like where he was fishing.

"I'm going to walk up the creek a little way and try it out. You stay right here," he said.

We fished for hours. I hadn't caught a thing but had gone through one bottle of eggs. Some older boys came down and started fishing by me. They probably thought I knew what I was doing. I kept throwing my line out, then reeling it back up. Nothing.

Lugnut came back carrying a Y shaped stick with three small fish on it and one Y shaped stick with nothing.

"How you doing?" he asked.

"Not so good. I don't think there's any fish living here. Can I move up to where you are?"

"No, the water is too fast up there. Just stay here. Don't worry. When they want to bite your hook, they will. I made you a fish carrier. Just take your fish off your hook and push the stick through their gills and out the mouth."

"Won't that hurt?"

Lugnut must not have heard me 'cause he just moved his head back and forth. Mumbled something. Then he walked off shaking his head.

I fished and I fished. Nothing. The older boys next to me kept catching fish. Then they'd put a stick through the fish's gill, out its mouth, and place it on the ground. I was frustrated. I was hungry. I was tired and my feet were soaked. I wanted to go home and build forts with the gang. Stupid fish. I never like to eat fish anyway. The older boys reeled in their line and headed up stream where Lugnut was fishing. But they left their fish on a stick.

I looked around. I didn't care. Lugnut was going to come back and ask me "How you doing" and I'd say "okay." No more. I parted the small brush that was between me and the other boys' fish. They were busy laughing and weren't paying any attention to me. I snuck over and took one. Just one little fish off the stick and put it on my stick. There. Now ask me. I dare you to ask me!

I kept fishing. Catching nothing. Lugnut came back with two of the older boys.

"How you doing?" Lugnut asked.

Not looking at him, I held up my stick with the one tiny fish on it.

"Hmmm, looks like you borrowed someone's fish. Why would you do that?"

How did he know. I looked at the fish. It looked like a fish. It didn't have a number or a name on it. How'd he know I borrowed that fish. I noticed the older boys standing behind Lugnut.

"Kenny saw you take it. Why would you steal. The creek is full of fish."

"I didn't steal. I borrowed. I was going to put it back, but I just felt kind of good having that fish on a stick watching me fish. I thought maybe it would bring me good luck. But I didn't mean to steal. I promise I didn't."

Lugnut turned to Kenny. "What do you think, Kenny?"

"My dad is the head of Fish and Game. He's also the magistrate judge, so maybe we should go talk with him and see what he thinks. Stealing fish is a serious offense and jail time might be involved," Kenny said with a straight face.

"I swear on the Starr Hill Gang's bible that I didn't mean to steal. I only meant to borrow. I promise to all the fishermen I will never borrow a fish again. I can't go to jail I have school tomorrow."

"Tell you what. I'll go home and talk with my dad the judge. If he says you have to come in, then your brother can bring you down to the jail. If I can convince him you only borrowed the fish, maybe he will forget it. It'll take a couple of days, so you'll just have to wait and see."

"Oh, thank you and thank the judge. I promise I'll never borrow again."

"Grab your pole," Lugnut said. "We have enough fish. Let's head up to the road and go home. Thanks, Kenny. We'll wait to hear from you or your dad."

"Hey, John, you might as well take your fish on the stick. You can keep it. Just don't do it again."

A couple of years went by before Lugnut took me fishing again. I don't think he wanted to be out in public with me. I wasn't a real thief. Just a fish borrower. Nothing serious. Unless you're a fisherman.

It was winter, and Lugnut had a 1949 two-door Chevy. Different from his "53" Chevy. But it still had the loudest pipes. It was cool. I loved going down the hills when he rapped those pipes off.

"Hey, you want to go ice fishing up at the Salmon Creek Dam?"

"Yea, when?"

"Right now. Just put on some warm clothes and your packs."

I like this fishing, 'cause I never had to carry a thing. Lugnut had a backpack with wood on the sides. Maybe for starting a fire or something.

We drove to the Salmon Creek Power House and parked. We headed up the trail which was a lot steeper than I thought It would be. The snow came up to the top of my boots. I tried to step in Lugnut's foot prints but they were too far apart. So, I'd step into one print then do a half step and back into his foot print again. Not easy. I made my own trail in the snow. We got to the bottom of the dam. Wow, it was huge. It was all cement. I'd never seen a dam before.

We climbed up the left side where the snow was packed down. Once we got on top, we headed toward the mouth of the dam right at the base of Mt. Juneau.

Lugnut said, "Let's try here, should be good."

The snow was now over my knees. It didn't bother Lugnut, his body was farther from the ground. Finally, we got there. Huffing and puffing, I settled my butt down into the snow.

He took off his backpack and started to empty it. There weren't any fishing poles. We marched all the way up here and forgot the fishing poles. I wasn't going to go back down and get them. Just when I was going to say something, he took out three metal poles and screwed them together. The one had a flat end like a hatchet.

"Let's clean off all the snow 'til we get down to the ice. Then I am going to use this ice, pick I made in Mr. Bibb's shop class."

We cleared the snow away, and Lugnut started chopping the ice. I got down on my knees. When he'd stop, I'd clean out all the ice pieces. Finally, he broke through the ice and water started to fill the hole.

"Grab the backpack and get the two pieces of wood with the fishing line wrapped around them. I'll try and get most of the ice out of the hole, then we can start fishing."

I opened the backpack and got out the wood with the fishing line. I'd never seen such a short fishing pole before. Sometimes I worried about Lugnut being all together upstairs. On the end of the fishing line, he put a hook. Took a jar of little eggs, same kind we'd used before. They had to be old by now. My hands were cold. I stuck them in my pants to warm up. He tried putting the eggs on the hook, but they'd split and fall off.

"You need to put a few of these eggs in your mouth to thaw them out. Don't swallow them, they're for the fish." Lugnut said.

Lugnut had some in his mouth as he telling me how to bait my hook. I took two out of the jar. Frozen solid. I looked them over and over. Lugnut already had his line down in the water moving the piece of wood up and down. He glanced up at me. I couldn't wait any longer. In they went. My mouth started to water as they thawed out. Then I felt like I had eaten Cream of Wheat. With the lumps. I swallowed. Both of them went down fast. I spit out what was left in my mouth. Just water.

"Hurry up, I got one on the line," Lugnet said. He pulled a six-inch trout out of the hole and let it flop on the snow.

Now I wanted to fish. Quickly I put a small handful in my mouth so in case I swallowed one or two I'd have some left over.

We caught twenty-four fish in one hour. It was two o'clock, so Lugnut started to pack things up.

"Let's go. It's going to be dark in another hour, and we don't want to be caught on the trail.

I started going fishing more often. As I got older, he took me out to Montana Creek about twelve miles out the road on the west side of Mendenhall Glacier. We used fishing poles on these trips, and it was a lot scarier. We'd park the car at the old saw mill. Walk for about ten minutes through skunk cabbage, ferns, and tall grass. Lugnut always led the way. He'd talk really loudly because that was supposed to scare the brown bears away. We'd get to the side of the creek, and he'd walk out into the middle looking for brown bear. If everything looked good, we'd fish.

I have been in the middle of the creek when a brown bear would be down the river from us.

"Don't stare at them. Just keep your eyes open in their direction. Don't make any sudden movement or sound. Let them walk up stream. Act like you're not here. Then we're going to slowly walk out of here," Lugnut whispered.

I didn't care for the bears being that close. They were bigger than I was. Probably not as smart, but, when you're that big, brains don't really matter.

*I never became a great fisherman,
but I looked like one.
Especially with borrowed fish.*

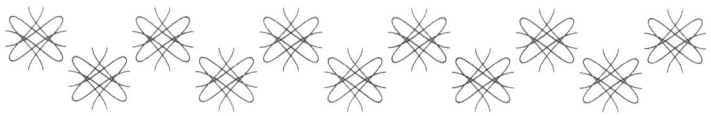

Holy Paddle

Second week in eighth grade, my confidence was still at the bottom of the totem pole. After trying to form a Starr Hill band a few years back, and failing, my singing skills had taken a nose dive. Mrs. Wagner, our music teacher, was a very strict teacher and was always trying to get me to sound more like a robin than a drowning frog. She was a stickler on boys participating, plus she only smiled when the sun was shining outside. Twice a year!

My buddy Bob and I decided to liven up the music class a little. Bob was one of those kids that was born gifted. He had a beard, and his knuckles dragged along the ground when he walked. He was definitely the biggest boy in class. No, the whole school. Maybe town.

We got the class laughing one day while Mrs. Wagner's back was turned. But like all teachers of that era, she had eyes that could see through the back of her head. Through all that hair.

She whirled around. "Bob and John, I want you two to head right over to the principal's office now! See if the principal thinks you're as funny as the class does."

We took our time. Telling jokes. Guessing what the principal might hand out for punishment. You know, the usual things you do on the way to a principal's office.

Mr. Leith didn't seem like a bad guy. He was from somewhere in America, and this was his first year as a principal in Alaska. He had already made some major changes in the school. For example, when girls sat in the gym, they had to put one ankle behind the other. Kind of silly, but okay. Boys had to wear belts. Some of us just put a piece of rope around our pants and tied it in front. Mr. Leith didn't have a problem with that. Bob and I felt he'd give us a short lecture and send us back to class.

We sat outside his office for at least an hour. The lady in the office must have been related to Mrs. Wagner.

Finally, Mr. Leith came through the door.

"Follow me boys and don't make a sound. Not one peep." He was carrying something wrapped in brown paper bag.

We slowly climbed the stairs and went through the double doors that led out to the balcony of the gymnasium. This was the old high school, so it had a huge gym. It was also the home of the Gold Medal Basketball games. A wonderful smell of sweat and excitement filled the air.

As we approached the railing, I noticed the whole school was sitting in the bleachers below us. Everyone was quiet. The girls all had one ankle behind the other, and everyone was peering up at us. I felt a little embarrassed. I wasn't used to all this attention.

"We're only two weeks into the school year," Mr. Leith said, "and already we have two boys who think they are smarter than the teacher."

He didn't say hi to the kids or anything. He got right to the point. I had a bad feeling this was not going to be good.

"No one is smarter than the teachers. Period. Except me. There are many ways to solve this problem but the best one is to show the school that this administration does not put up with this kind of misconduct."

He slowly raised the brown paper package and unwrapped it.

Oh my god!!!

It was the biggest paddle I'd ever seen. It must have been an inch thick and had three, yes three holes, drilled into it so there wouldn't be any wind resistance on the way to your butt. The bright gymnasium lights made it look like gold. I'd only read about these paddles. Now I had the feeling it was going to be more than that. My knees started to weaken. I was growing shorter in front of the whole class. Small beads of sweat ran down into my eyes. I glanced over at Bob. His knuckles were gently resting on the floor, and he seemed to be whistling. Silently.

"Mr. Bob, bend over and grab the railing."

I wonder if they called the victim that was about to hanged "Mr." It seemed too formal. Why call someone "Mr." if you going to kill them? I had a bad feeling that's what was going to happen to Bob and me.

Bob bent over and grabbed the railing. Mr. Leith held the paddle up so the whole school could marvel at it. He then took a baseball swing at Bob's butt.

Whack! The sound echoed like a gunshot. Made the hairs in my ears vibrate.

Whop! You could hear the air going through those three holes make a high shrieking sound like fingernails on a black board. Bob didn't flinch. He was like a marble statue.

Wham! How many is that? Three, but it seemed like ten or twelve. Bob just stared straight ahead. He straightens up and steps back to where I was standing.

"Mr. John. Grab the railing."

I didn't have to bend over. I had to reach up. There was smell of burning rubber in the air. Was that Bob's butt or my tennis shoes melting into the floor.

Wham! I didn't hear it, but I felt it all over my body. Quickly dry tears filled my eyes. Remember Bob didn't show any sign of pain. I can't either. I had to think of something so I wouldn't cry. How about Sue?

She just broke—

Whop! My spine rattled like a xylophone.

The third wallop I don't remember. All I knew was that I wasn't going to be the wise guy any more. My body just couldn't take this. I tried stepping back, but my legs weren't attached to my butt any longer.

Mr. Leith held up the paddle.

"You may all return to your classes. Let's try to obey our teachers, and we won't have another one of these assemblies."

He slowly walked off. Didn't even look our way or say goodbye. Not even, you are brave boys; *we need more like you.* Nothing.

I looked at Bob. He had a smirk on his face. I could only dream of being that tough.

After that day, Bob became a legend.
I became a soprano.

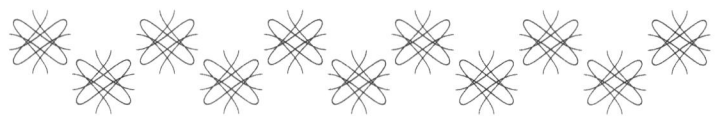

Epilogue

I don't know if we were brave or just dumb, but somehow, we survived with all our fingers, most of our common sense, and a few scars we still brag about. Starr Hill taught us how to laugh, how to scrape our knees, and how to grow up without really meaning to. If you're ever in Juneau and you hear some kids yelling in the trees, don't worry. That's just the next gang figuring out the world their own way. Lucky them.

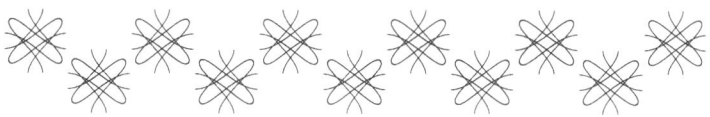

Acknowledgments

Writing this book was never a solo adventure. Just like the Starr Hill Gang, it took a whole crew of friends, family, and encouragers to make it happen. I want to take a moment to thank the people who helped me along the way.

First, my deepest thanks to Sarah Shepard. I enrolled in her memoir writing class without the foggiest idea of what lay ahead. She gave me the tools, the guidance, and—most of all—the encouragement to start turning memories into stories. Without Sarah, Little Johnny might still be hiding in the attic instead of marching onto a page.

In that same class, I met Barbara Maier, a playwright with a sharp ear for dialogue. Barbara helped me keep the voices of the Starr Hill Gang alive and young...never letting them grow old or lose the spark of mischief that made them who they were.

Not long after, I was fortunate to meet Mitch Nelson, a classic storyteller who became a mentor to me. We'd sit and talk about a character or a story, turning it around to see it from different angles and through different eyes. I have learned so much from him, and his wisdom and perspective helped me bring more depth—and more mischief—into these pages.

And then came Karen Munson. She was convinced I must have stopped taking English in the fourth grade. Her pages came back covered in so many red marks it looked like a beautiful sunset. But she was the one who made sure this book could walk, run, and fly...and it did all three. Without her, these stories might never have left the runway.

All I need now was to publish this and be off to the races. That's when I met Marcia Breece, an accomplished author who took me under her wing and guided me through the maze of publishing. Without her help, this book might still be circling the track while I paced back and forth, tugging on the few hair strands I have left.

A special gratitude goes to Doc Eide, my best friend from second grade on. We played toy soldiers, rolled in dog poop, swam in the Evergreen pool, and caused more than a little trouble for the teachers. He belonged to the "Sixth Street Gang," just a few blocks from the Starr Hill Gang. His dad—a professional photographer—took the picture on the front cover of this book. Back then the Starr Hill Gang was usually in timeout so we never got our picture taken, so it's a wonder we ever got one.

Thank you, Doc, for the lasting friendship and the photo.

Now came the hard part. How do you thank your mom and dad, Aileen and Bert, who have long since passed on? Without them, and without their patience and persistence, there never would have been a Little Johnny. They gave me the grounding to explore, the freedom to imagine, and the encouragement to turn scraped knees and wild schemes into stories worth telling. This book carries their fingerprints, even if you can't see them on the page.

Now come the two most important people: my sister Carla—better known as Blister—and our older brother Wayne—better known as Lugnut. These two make up the book...the core, the laughs, and the crying. Every wild plan, every scraped knee, every triumph and disaster...we shared together. My admiration for those two grows every minute of every day. This book may have my name on the cover, but Blister and Lugnut live in every page.

To my wife, Susan...the most important thank you of all. Thank you for putting up with me, for correcting me, for calming me down when the stories (or I) ran off the rails. You've been my steady hand, my editor, and my safe harbor through it all. Without you, this book would never have made it into the world.

And one last thanks goes to all the kids who ever lived on Starr Hill and knew the joy of its camaraderie. Whether we were building forts, playing ball in the Chicken Yard, or just dreaming bigger than the hill itself, you were part of the spirit that carried me through these stories. This book is for you, too.

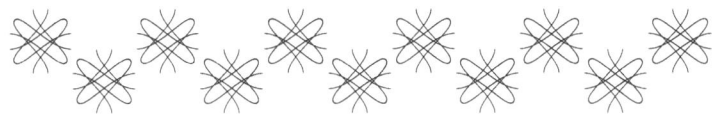

About the Author

I was born in Juneau, Alaska, and spent the next sixty years surrounded by its mountains, rain, and mischief. These days I make my home in Sequim, Washington, with my loving wife—my first love in this book, and my last in life.

Over the years, I've explored a few creative detours. I co-wrote the play *The Man in the Green Truck*, developed two games, *Up and Down the River* and *Whales*, with help from some close friends, and even dabbled in driftwood and resin art shown at the Blue Whole Gallery in Sequim.

Whether it's writing, storytelling, or creating something new, my goal has always been simple, to put a smile on people's faces and maybe give them a reason to laugh along the way.

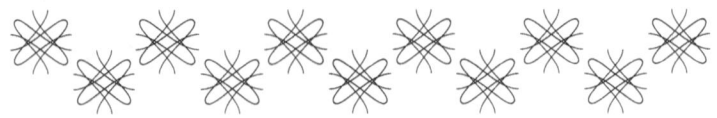

Praise for I Survived the Star Hill Gang

Time travel is real! Just open this book and read. You'll be transported back to 1950's Alaska led by a master storyteller and guide.

Little Johnny tells it like it is for a young boy growing up in Alaska way back in the day. Things were different back then. People? Not so much. We all know the Starr Hill Gang. They have different names in our lives, but they're all around us. Little Johnny points then out just by telling us about his friends.

When you return, the world will be different. Little Johnny reminds us what it's like seeing the world for the first time...again.

— Mitch Nelson: Professional Storyteller,
  Song Writer, Singer, and Harmonica Player.

Hey! This book was written by John, who grew up in Alaska before it was even a state. He did all kinds of wild stuff—like hiding a pigeon in his room and playing outside when it was so cold snot froze! Johnny tells his stories like he's talking

right at you. He says things like, "I didn't mean to fall off the chair onto the stove. I just had to see the popcorn pop!" Even the hospital nurse knows his name. His stories make me think about those days when friends were the best thing ever. If you've never been to Alaska, Johnny shows you how to have fun even when all you've got is rain or snow. It's an adventure every time you turn a page!
— Barbara Jo Maier, friend and co-author of
The Man in the Green Truck. A memoir written by John and dramatized into Readers Theatre

I Survived the Star Hill Gang is a beautiful book: heartfelt, compelling, funny, full of suspense, and mostly, love. The dialogue is superb. John Bertholl writes and thinks like a little boy growing up in the wilds of Alaska. Well, Juneau anyway. I loved every minute I spent reading this book. The story is funny and satisfyingly, surprising."
— Sarah Shepard, Writing Instructor, Writing Your Life: Creative Memoir, Peninsula College

Starr Hill from our front porch

www.ingramcontent.com/pod-product-compliance
Lightning Source LLC
Chambersburg PA
CBHW070135080526
44586CB00015B/1697